SHEPHERD'S NOTES

Shepherd's Notes Titles Available

SHEPHERD'S NOTES COMMENTARY SERIES

Old Testament

9-780-805-490-282 Genesis
9-780-805-490-565 Exodus
9-780-805-490-695 Leviticus, Numbers
9-780-805-490-275 Deuteronomy
9-780-805-490-589 Joshua, Judges
9-780-805-490-572 Ruth, Esther
9-780-805-490-633 1 & 2 Samuel
9-780-805-490-077 1 & 2 Kings
9-780-805-490-649 1 & 2 Chronicles
9-780-805-491-944 Ezra, Nehemiah
9-780-805-490-060 Job
9-780-805-493-399 Psalms 1-50

9-780-805-493-405 Psalms 51-100
9-780-805-493-412 Psalms 101-150
9-780-805-490-169 Proverbs
9-780-805-490-596 Ecclesiastes, Song of Solomon
9-780-805-491-975 Isaiah
9-780-805-490-701 Jeremiah, Lamentations
9-780-805-490-787 Ezekiel
9-780-805-490-152 Daniel
9-780-805-493-269 Hosea, Obadiah
9-780-805-493-344 Jonah, Zephaniah
9-780-805-490-657 Haggai, Malachi

New Testament

9-781-558-196-889 Matthew
9-780-805-490-718 Mark
9-780-805-490-046 Luke
9-781-558-196-933 John
9-781-558-196-919 Acts
9-780-805-490-053 Romans
9-780-805-493-252 1 Corinthians
9-780-805-493-351 2 Corinthians
9-781-558-196-902 Galatians
9-780-805-493-276 Ephesians

9-781-558-196-896 Philippians, Colossians, Philemon
9-780-805-490-008 1 & 2 Thessalonians
9-781-558-196-926 1 & 2 Timothy, Titus
9-780-805-493-368 Hebrews
9-780-805-490-183 James
9-780-805-490-190 1 & 2 Peter & Jude
9-780-805-492-149 1, 2 & 3 John
9-780-805-490-176 Revelation

SHEPHERD'S NOTES CHRISTIAN CLASSICS

9-780-805-493-474 *Mere Christianity,* C. S. Lewis
9-780-805-493-535 *The Problem of Pain/ A Grief Observed,* C. S. Lewis
9-780-805-491-999 *The Confessions,* Augustine
9-780-805-492-002 *Calvin's Institutes*
9-780-805-493-948 *Miracles,* C. S. Lewis

9-780-805-491-968 *Lectures to My Students,* Charles Haddon Spurgeon
9-780-805-492-200 *The Writings of Justin Martyr*
9-780-805-493-450 *The City of God,* Augustine
9-780-805-491-982 *The Cost of Discipleship,* Bonhoeffer

SHEPHERD'S NOTES — BIBLE SUMMARY SERIES

9-780-805-493-771 Old Testament
9-780-805-493-788 New Testament

9-780-805-493-849 Life & Teachings of Jesus
9-780-805-493-856 Life & Letters of Paul

SHEPHERD'S NOTES

When you need a guide through the Scriptures

Job

HOLMAN
REFERENCE

NASHVILLE, TENNESSEE

Shepherd's Notes—*Job*
© 1998
by Broadman & Holman Publishers
Nashville, Tennessee
All rights reserved
Printed in the United States of America

978–0–8054–9006–0
Dewey Decimal Classification: 223.10
Subject Heading: BIBLE. O.T. JOB
Library of Congress Card Catalog Number: 97–49998

Library of Congress Cataloging-in-Publication Data

Job / Duane A. Garrett, editor
      p. cm. — (Shepherd's notes)
    Includes bibliographical references.
    ISBN 0–8054–9006–X
    1. Bible. O.T. Job—Study and teaching. I. Garrett, Duane A. II. Series
BS1415.5J63   1997
223'.107—dc21

                         97–49998
                           CIP

5 6 7 8 9 10 11 12 13   14 13 12 11 10 09

CONTENTS

Dear Reader:

Shepherd's Notes are designed to give you a quick, step-by-step overview of every book of the Bible. They are not meant to be substitutes for the biblical text; rather, they are study guides intended to help you explore the wisdom of Scripture in personal or group study and to apply that wisdom successfully in your own life.

Shepherd's Notes guide you through the main themes of each book of the Bible and illuminate fascinating details through appropriate commentary and reference notes. Historical and cultural background information brings the Bible into sharper focus.

Six different icons, used throughout the series, call your attention to historical-cultural information, Old Testament and New Testament references, word pictures, unit summaries, and personal applications for everyday life.

Whether you are a novice or a veteran at Bible study, I believe you will find *Shepherd's Notes* a resource that will take you to a new level in your mining and applying the riches of Scripture.

In Him,

David R. Shepherd
Editor-in-Chief

HOW TO USE THIS BOOK

DESIGNED FOR THE BUSY USER

Shepherd's Notes for Job is designed to provide an easy-to-use tool for getting a quick handle on this significant Bible book's, important features, and for gaining an understanding of its message. Information available in more difficult-to-use reference works has been incorporated into the *Shepherd's Notes* format. This brings you the benefits of many advanced and expensive works packed into one small volume.

Shepherd's Notes are for laymen, pastors, teachers, small-group leaders and participants, as well as the classroom student. Enrich your personal study or quiet time. Shorten your class or small-group preparation time as you gain valuable insights into the truths of God's Word that you can pass along to your students or group members.

DESIGNED FOR QUICK ACCESS

Bible students with time constraints will especially appreciate the timesaving features built into the *Shepherd's Notes*. All features are intended to aid a quick and concise encounter with the heart of the messages of Job.

Concise Commentary. Short sections provide quick "snapshots" of the narrative and themes of this book, highlighting important points and other information.

Outlined Text. Comprehensive outlines cover the entire texts of Job. This is a valuable feature for following the narrative's flow, allowing for a quick, easy way to locate a particular passage.

Shepherd's Notes. These summary statements or capsule thoughts appear at the close of every key section of the narrative. While functioning in part as a quick summary, they also deliver the essence of the message presented in the sections which they cover.

Icons. Various icons in the margin highlight recurring themes in the book of Job, aiding in selective searching or tracing of those themes.

Sidebars and Charts. These specially selected features provide additional background information to your study or preparation. Charts offer a quick overview of important subjects. Sidebars include definitions as well as cultural, historical, and biblical insights.

Maps. These are placed at appropriate places in the book to aid your understanding and study of a text or passage.

Questions to Guide Your Study. These thought-provoking questions and discussion starters are designed to encourage interaction with the truth and principles of God's Word.

DESIGNED TO WORK FOR YOU

Personal Study. Using *Shepherd's Notes* with a passage of Scripture can enlighten your study and take it to a new level. At your fingertips is information that would require searching several volumes to find. In addition, many points of application occur throughout the volume, contributing to personal growth.

Teaching. Outlines frame the texts of Job, providing a logical presentation of its message. Capsule thoughts designated as "Shepherd's Notes" provide summary statements for presenting the essence of key points and events. Application icons point out personal application of the messages of this book. Historical Context icons indicate where cultural and historical background information is supplied.

Group Study. *Shepherd's Notes* can be an excellent companion volume to use for gaining a quick but accurate understanding of the messages of Job. Each group member can benefit by having his or her own copy. The *Notes'* format accommodates the study of themes throughout Job. Leaders may use its flexible features to prepare for group sessions or use them during group sessions. Questions to guide your study can spark discussion of Job's key points and truths to be discovered in this delightful book.

LIST OF MARGIN ICONS USED IN JOB

 Shepherd's Notes. Placed at the end of each section, a capsule statement provides the reader with the essence of the message of that section.

 Old Testament Reference. Used when the writer refers to Old Testament passages or when Old Testament passages illuminate a text.

 New Testament Reference. Used when the writer refers to New Testament passages that are related to or have a bearing on the passage's understanding or interpretation.

 Historical Background. To indicate historical, cultural, geographical, or biographical information that sheds light on the understanding or interpretation of a passage.

 Personal Application. Used when the text provides a personal or universal application of truth.

 Word Picture. Indicates that the meaning of a specific word or phrase is illustrated so as to shed light on it.

INTRODUCTION

The book of Job sometimes disappoints its readers. This is not because something is wrong with the book. People come to it with the idea that it will explain to them why their lives are going so badly. They have heard somewhere that Job deals with the problem of "why people suffer," and in Job they look at least for solace if not also for answers. Expecting some kind of wise and wonderful words that will both comfort and heal, they find themselves instead in the midst of a tempest of a bewildering debate between Job and his friends. The speeches go off on tangents that, to many modern readers, have no real purpose. After laboring through the charges and countercharges of Job and his companions, these readers may be forgiven for naively assuming that when they come to God's speech they will at last have something that will answer all their questions. But here the disappointment is greatest of all. God seems to do little more than berate Job with an overwhelming series of questions, all aimed at proving that Job does not have the ability to govern the world. Strangely, however, Job finds this bombast to be a complete and altogether satisfactory answer to his concerns, and he humbly bows his head before God.

Do we serve God because He will reward us if we do and punish us if we do not? If so, what about cases where the wicked prosper and the good suffer? Could there be another reason to serve Him?

What are we to make of all this? The world of Job turns out to be a very alien place, and whatever answers it provides do not seem to work for us. Actually, the book of Job answers the most profound of questions, but we must understand what those questions are. Job does not answer the question: Why do bad things happen to good people? It deals with an even more basic concern: Why should a person serve God? Or, to hear the question as spoken by Satan, the protagonist of the whole book, "Does Job fear God for nothing?" (1:9, NRSV). Or again, to hear it in the mouth of the anguished hero of the book, "Who is the Almighty, that we should serve Him? And what profit do we have if we pray to Him?" (21:15, NRSV).

Another fundamental issue of the book of Job is the whole issue of whether God governs the world justly. Job, an altogether innocent man, suffers unimaginable loss and pain. In fact, he receives in full the kind of punishment that is supposed to be inflicted on the wicked. Where then is God's justice? Job's companions in the book will assert that God's justice never misfires. If Job has been punished, then Job is a sinner. Job himself, however, refuses to accept this solution. He knows he is not guilty. More than that, he can point to many examples of the guilty avoiding all punishment (chap. 21).

BASIC STORY AND OUTLINE

Basic Story

Where is the justice of God? and, What are the reasons for serving God? are the questions that the book seeks to answer. To read the book without keeping these questions in mind is to risk misreading it entirely.

The book tells us that there was a man by the name of Job whom God considered to be so fine an example of purity that He could hold him up before the accuser, Satan himself, as one above reproach. Satan responded that Job was only righteous because God had protected him from trouble, and if God were to take away his riches, health, and family, he would become as bad a sinner as anyone else. God then allowed Satan to test Job by removing all his possessions and killing all his children. For all this, however, Job did not "curse God"; that is, he did not renounce his allegiance to God. Satan then demanded that he be allowed to take away Job's health as well, and Satan was granted permission to afflict him with painful boils. Still, Job persisted in his piety.

At this point, Job's three friends (Eliphaz, Bildad, and Zophar) arrived in order to comfort him in his distress. They are soon dismayed, however, at Job's insistence that he had done no iniquity that merited this kind of punishment, and with increasing anger and vehemence they tried to prove to him that he was a sinner and that what God had done to him was completely fair. The debate ended with no resolution, but a fifth, hitherto unannounced character named Elihu suddenly spoke up and claimed that he could resolve the problem of Job's suffering. He too failed, and God Himself then appeared and addressed Job. The suffering patriarch recognized his error and repented before God, but to the readers' surprise this did not vindicate the friends. God severely censured them, and Job had to intercede in order for them to be forgiven. As for Job himself, God restored to him his health and fortunes.

Satan

Satan is the transliteration of the Hebrew word meaning "adversary."

Outline of the Book

The structure of the book is quite straightforward. After the prologue, Job and his friends debate in three cycles of speeches. These are followed by a poem on wisdom, Job's final speech, the Elihu speeches, God's speeches, and an epilogue. The outline is as follows:

I. Prologue (1:1–2:13)
   A. Background of the Story (1:1–5)
   B. First Episode (1:6–22)
   C. Second Episode (2:1–10)
   D. Background of the Dialogue (2:11–13)
II. First Cycle (3:1–11:20)

BACKGROUND, UNITY, AND GENRE OF THE BOOK

Date and Authorship

The book of Job is anonymous. No one knows when or by whom it was written; no sources for

Job have been uncovered; and no other book of the Bible gives us any information about where the book of Job came from. (Ezekiel 14:14, 20 does mention the man Job, but this does not tell us anything about the origin of the book.) Some have suggested it was written in the Babylonian exile, but the book does not allude to that or any event from Israel's history. We should also add that Job says nothing about the institutions of Israel, such as the covenants or the Levitical priesthood. This, too, tells us nothing, however, about when the book was written. Even if the book represents an era prior to Abraham himself, as some have suggested, that does not mean it was *written* that early.

Scholars have debated over whether the language of the book tells us anything about when it was written. Some scholars argue that there are loan words from other languages in the book and that these can be used to help establish the date of its composition. At present, however, it is safe to say that no one has been able to settle the issue of the book's date conclusively by this method.

Integrity and Unity

Many scholars believe that the book of Job as we have it today was written in stages by many authors or editors and that it was not the product of a single mind or even a single outlook. They contend that portions of the book are later additions—that is, that they were not written by the original author and are not true to his intentions. The prologue, epilogue, and Elihu speeches are often regarded as secondary, with the speeches by Job, the three friends, and God constituting the original core of the book. A frequent criticism is that Job 1–2 with its focus on Satan represents later Jewish theology and that

Ezekiel 14:14, 20 does mention the man Job: "'Even though these three men, Noah, Daniel, and Job were in its midst, by their own righteousness they could only deliver themselves," declares the Lord (v. 14, NASB). Ezekiel's reference doesn't tell us anything about when and where Job was written.

Loan Word

Sometimes one language will simply adopt a word from another language; English has adopted many words from French, such as *sang-froid*. One occasionally finds words from Aramaic, Persian, Greek, or other languages in the Hebrew Bible.

Job does allude to other biblical passages, especially Gen. 1–3 and certain psalms of David. Job 7:17–21 seems to be based on Psalm 8. This implies that it was written after David. A good possibility is that the book appeared in the reign of either Solomon or Hezekiah, both of whom encouraged the study of wisdom literature.

this contrasts with the dialogues, which never mention Satan. Thus, some assert that the prologue to Job is a later addition. Another common argument is that the Elihu speeches must have been written by a pious Israelite who was offended at much of what Job had to say and who felt a need to answer Job and give the book a more orthodox conclusion.

But these opinions do little to enhance the reader's task of interpreting Job. The book makes no sense if the prologue and epilogue are deleted, and the Elihu speeches are essential to the plan of the book (see commentary). We cannot interpret Job by omitting difficult or unusual chapters. As we shall attempt to show, all of Job works together to convey a unified message, and what seems to be awkward or inconsistent actually is intentional and necessary for developing that message. For example, the apparent disappearance of Satan after chapter 2 is actually a very important point in the unfolding of the book. It is not a matter of two different authors being at work but of a single author of genius being at work.

The Genre of Job

Job is a book unlike any other, inside or outside of the Bible. It does, however, have many features that are found in other books. Quite a number of books from Egypt and Mesopotamia bewail the suffering of humanity and have some parallels to Job.

Job also has many similarities to other books of the Old Testament. No single book is exactly like Job, but one can find elements in Job that are quite similar to what we see elsewhere. Examples are as follows:

Hymn. The book has many psalmlike hymns that praise God for His power and justice (e.g., 5:9–16 and 26:5–14). See Psalms 94 and 97.

Proverb. The speakers often use pithy sayings to make their points or to appeal to traditional wisdom. One can compare Job 5:2 to Proverbs 29:11 and Job 28:28 to Proverbs 1:7.

Lamentation. Job repeatedly bewails what has befallen him, as in 3:1–26; 6:2–7; 10:1–12; 19:1–21. We see similar passages in Psalm 22:1–18 and the entire book of Lamentations.

The Protests of the Eloquent Peasant, an Egyptian work from the second millennium B.C., is often compared to Job for the pathos with which it describes human distress. Still, this and other such books do not compare to Job for the way it grapples with the most fundamental questions about God, humanity, and justice.

Questioning of Traditions. Job sometimes bluntly challenged conventional wisdom. One can compare his outburst in 21:17–19 to Ecclesiastes 9:2–3.

Wisdom Poem. Job has several lengthy poems on the value of wisdom and right behavior. One can compare Job 28 to Proverbs 30:2–4 and Job 8:11–22 to Psalm 1:3–6.

Prophetic Ecstasy. The friends sometimes claimed to have had prophetic visions and revelations. See Job 4:12–14 and 32:18–20 and compare Isaiah 6.

These and other types of literature are found both in Job and in other books of the Bible. Once again, however, Job cannot be identified with these other types of books. It is not a book of lamentations, or of prophecy, or of psaltery, or of proverbial wisdom. It is in a class by itself. It does, however, have a surprising number of similarities to one other type of biblical literature: apocalyptic.

Job and Apocalyptic Literature
Apocalyptic is a type of literature in the Bible that encourages believers to persevere in faith in the

face of persecution or evil. It often uses fantastic animals or visions, and it gives the heavenly reality of the triumph of God that contradicts the earthly semblance of reality that the power of evil is victorious.

Few readers (or scholars) have recognized the close affinity between the book of Job and apocalyptic literature.

One normally does not think of Job, a book associated with wisdom literature, when thinking of apocalyptic sources. When we look at the characteristics of apocalyptic literature, however, Job seems to have all of them. The characteristics that Job and apocalyptic literature share are as follows:

1. Both deal with historical reality on two levels: the heavenly and the earthly. Apocalyptic asserts that behind the conflicts on earth are conflicts between God and Satan in heaven, as does Job 1–2.

2. Apocalyptic often includes a cataclysmic undoing of creation, as does Job 3 (see comments on that chapter).

3. Apocalyptic deals in special numbers, especially three and seven (e.g., Revelation has seven seals, seven trumpets, and seven bowls—three series of seven). Job, too, makes heavy use of these numbers. For example, there are seven days of silence before the dialogue begins and then three rounds of debate between Job and his three friends. Also, Job makes a "negative confession" of fourteen (= 2 x 7) sins in 31:1–40. Hence, the numbers three and seven are surprisingly prominent in Job.

4. Apocalyptic acknowledges the reader's inability to decipher the meaning of the text and calls him or her to deeper understanding, as in Matthew 24:15. The Elihu speeches serve this function (see comments).

5. Apocalyptic uses fantastic or mythological animals as symbols to get its message across, as Daniel 7:1–8 does with the four beasts. In His speech in Job, God uses a series of descriptions of wild animals to make His point to Job, and He climaxes His speech with accounts of Behemoth and Leviathan in Job 40:15–41:34.

6. Apocalyptic sometimes contains a doxological intermission both to break the tension of the conflict and as a signal that the divine intervention is soon to begin. Revelation 19:1–10, a doxology that comes in between the fall of Babylon and the fury of the rider on the white horse, has this function. Job 28, a poem in praise of wisdom, seems to have a similar function.

7. In Apocalyptic, divine intervention concludes the conflict. The same is obviously true of Job, where the sudden appearance of God in a whirlwind puts an end to all debating.

8. Apocalyptic calls the believer to endurance in the face of severe and inscrutable suffering. The whole of Job is a test of one believer's ability to withstand horrible calamity at the hands of Satan and persevere in his piety.

9. Apocalyptic concludes with the faithful believer having entered bliss. Job ends

with the patriarch vindicated and his fortunes restored.

THE MESSAGE OF JOB

It is impossible to describe the message of Job without working through the text. The brief discussion here is meant to anticipate the message of Job rather than describe it; full analysis of the message comes in the comments that follow. But one can say this: The message of Job is determined by the questions it seeks to answer. As stated above, the questions are: Does God govern justly? and, Why serve God? The answer the three friends provide is straightforward: "Yes, God governs justly because everyone is a sinner and He never punishes someone unless that person is wicked; and yes, one should serve God because those who serve Him have happy, prosperous lives, but those who do not serve Him suffer the consequences."

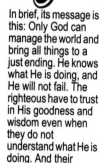

In brief, its message is this: Only God can manage the world and bring all things to a just ending. He knows what He is doing, and He will not fail. The righteous have to trust in His goodness and wisdom even when they do not understand what He is doing. And their greatest reward is simply this, that they know God.

This turns out to be a poor answer. In fact, it is similar to Satan's understanding of how things operate, that the righteous are righteous only because they do not want to lose the benefits of wealth and health (Job 1:9–10). The whole of the book of Job has the purpose of providing the right answers to those questions.

There is, however, a subtheme to the book of Job that quietly develops within the text. This is the fact that the reconciling of God and humanity ultimately requires a heavenly Redeemer who can overcome death and address both God and people as equals. There is, as the book strains to point out, a great gulf between God and humans, and only the Intercessor can bridge that gulf. This book of God, humanity, and justice is not complete without the Messiah.

QUESTIONS TO GUIDE YOUR STUDY

1. What are some of the key issues dealt with in the book of Job?
2. What do we know about who wrote Job and when and where it was written?
3. How important are the prologue and epilogue to the meaning of the book of Job?
4. What is *apocalyptic*, and what elements does Job have that are similar to apocalyptic writings?

COMMENTS ON THE TEXT

PROLOGUE (1:1–2:13)

This text, like 42:7–17, is written in prose. This distinguishes these two passages from all the rest of the book, which is poetry. Also, the opening and closing of the book are third person narrative; but all the rest, 3:1–42:6, is made up of the speeches by the various characters (Job, Eliphaz, Bildad, Zophar, Elihu, and God). Thus, it is conventional to speak of 1:1–2:13 as the "prologue" and 42:7–17 as the "epilogue."

The outline of this passage demonstrates the skill of its author. It is made up of two parallel episodes bounded by an "inclusion" structure. The outline of the text is as follows:

Inclusion

Ancient writers had techniques for telling stories. One such technique is "inclusion," a literary device in which the beginning and ending of a passage are similar to each other. Where inclusion occurs, it forms the boundaries of a passage.

   A. Background of the Story (1:1–5)

First Episode (1:6–22)
   B. Dialogue in Heaven (1:6–12)
   C. Affliction of Job (1:13–19)
   D. Job's Response (1:20–22)

Second Episode (2:1–10)
   B. Dialogue in Heaven (2:1–6)
   C. Affliction of Job (2:7–8)
   D. Job's Response (2:9–10)

Background of the Dialogue (2:11–13)

In this text, 1:1–5 prepares us for the initial story and 2:11–13 prepares us for the dialogues. The two episodes of the prologue (1:6–22; 2:1–10) parallel each other. Each begins with a dialogue in heaven in which Satan demands and receives from God qualified permission to afflict Job. After this, Satan brings various calamities upon the hapless hero, and then the text tells how Job responds to what has befallen him.

Job is declared to have been from "Uz."

"Uz"

Uz is a place that may have been near Edom and Philistia, south of Judah (see Lam. 4:21; Jer. 25:20). On the other hand, 1:3 declares that he was greatest of the men from the "east" which, for an Israelite reader, would have meant somewhere to the east of the Jordan Valley, and there is some basis for connecting Uz with the territory of Aram (Syria), northeast of Israel. Thus, Job may be placed either near Edom or in Syria, but not in Israel.

From the very beginning, we confront a peculiarity about the book of Job in the Old Testament context: It makes no reference to Israel, to the covenant between Israel and God, or to any aspects of Israelite religion. It is also noteworthy that the word LORD (*Yahweh*), the covenant name of Israel's God, appears 32 times in Job, but all of these are in chapters 1–2 and 40–42, with a single exception in 12:9. The dialogue thus removes itself from the story of Israel's faith and presents us with what is almost a philosophical discussion.

The opening verse also gives us one other important piece of information: Job was "blameless and upright," and he "feared God and turned away from evil." The reader, in order to understand this book, must always keep this piece of information in mind. Job did not suffer because he was evil, because he had some important lessons to learn, or because he in any sense needed chastisement as a spiritual discipline. Job was blameless. Too often interpreters are frustrated by their inability to resolve the enigmas posed by this book and unwittingly fall into the error of Job's three friends. They argue that Job must have somehow been at fault, and thus, in some manner he deserved his adversity. The opening verse could hardly have stated it more directly, however. Job feared God to the uttermost. Furthermore, as the rest of the prologue indicates, all of Job's afflictions came upon him *because of his great righteousness*, not because of any character flaw on his part.

The book fills out the picture of Job's great wealth and profound piety in 1:2–5. It is peculiar that Job had such an enormous number of camels and donkeys (3,000 of the former and 500 of the latter). He was not a nomad, because 1:14 tells us that he had farmland under tillage. Possibly he was a wealthy trader who sent caravans across the ancient world. Out of his reverence for God, he regularly offered sacrifices on behalf of his children after they had enjoyed a feast on the mere possibility that one had "cursed God." Cursing God is the very thing Satan says Job himself will do if God ceases protecting him (1:11).

In the first episode (1:6–22), God is in heaven with all of His angels, the host that surrounds His throne (Ps. 89:5–7). Like any king of the ancient Near East, God is here portrayed as holding court with His nobles and advisers. Some interpreters thus regard Satan in this book not as an evil character but as a kind of official prosecutor for the crown, charged with the task of seeking out those who offend the divine majesty. That is, in accusing Job, Satan is only doing his assigned task as a loyal servant of God. This interpretation, however, is a rather inept reading of the book. It is difficult to miss the malice with which Satan speaks to God and afflicts Job. He is cynical about Job's piety (1:9–11) and eager to do Job as much harm as

Curse

Strangely, the Hebrew text in 1:5 and 1:11 actually says "bless God" where translators have rendered it "curse God." This is not a translation error, however. The Hebrew text here uses an euphemism to avoid the terrible expression "curse God," but curse is still the meaning.

possible. An official prosecutor should not be so vindictive.

At the same time, we must note that Satan is at all times subordinate to God and can only act with God's permission. Some Christians give the devil too much due, as though he were autonomous and all but equal to God in power. This is dualism, not Christianity, and one should soundly reject the kind of "spiritual warfare" theology that falls into dualism.

Having received permission to take away all that Job possessed but not touch his person, Satan removed everything Job had, including his children. The raiders who plundered Job's possessions came from surprisingly diverse places.

The text emphasizes the outrageous, incomprehensible nature of Job's afflictions. In addition, it asserts that the sheep were destroyed by the "fire of God" (1:16). The expression calls to mind the fire that fell on Sodom (Gen. 19:24) and would lead the casual observer to conclude that Job was indeed a terrible sinner.

Here, we already see the distinction between the earthly, apparent (but false) reality, that God is displeased with Job, and the revealed reality of apocalyptic, that Job is suffering not because of his sin but because of his goodness. Having seen the heavenly interview, the reader knows the real reason for Job's extraordinary calamities; the characters of the story, who cannot see past the veil of earthly appearances, know nothing of this.

Job's response to the first calamity (1:21–22) is a model of piety. He submits and declares that all he had was from God anyway, that He had the right to take it back. In declaring that God's

Dualism

In theology, this is the idea that two principles or divine beings govern the universe, the one being good and the other evil. It is rejected by the Bible, which always treats Satan not as an *equal* but as a wicked *creature* of God who still must yield to God's authority.

May the name of the LORD be blessed

This expression describes submission to the rule of God and thanks for His benefits. It is the opposite of an expression of anger toward God.

name was blessed, Job gives a prayer of thanksgiving and compliance. The phrase appears in Psalm 113:2, a text that celebrates the LORD's sovereignty over all the earth as well as His compassion for the weak and afflicted. It also occurs in 1 Chronicles 17:27, where David thanks God for choosing his family line to be the means by which God would extend His reign over all the earth. Like these other prayers, Job's implies both submission and gratitude.

In the heavenly dialogue of the second episode (2:1–6), Satan contends that it was only because Job escaped without any physical harm that he was willing to continue to maintain an attitude of superficial devotion. Satan's expression in 2:4, "Skin for skin!" appears only here in the Bible.

"Skin for skin"

Although we cannot be certain of its meaning, it is obviously similar to the more famous proverb, "An eye for an eye and a tooth for a tooth," which implies that the only thing that equals the value of an eye is another eye (and thus that one who puts out someone else's eye should forfeit one's own). Therefore, "skin for skin" seems to mean that a man values nothing so much as his own skin and that Job could accept every other disaster so long as his own health was not touched.

The skin disease with which Satan afflicted Job was particularly cruel. He was apparently covered with boils and oozing sores. This would have been extremely painful, but it would neither be fatal nor render him delirious or mentally incapacitated. Thus, he would experience the full fury of his pain but have no reason to suppose that it would soon all be over, and he would not lose the ability to brood over why all this had happened to him. That is, his consciousness of his condition was part of his affliction. Job elsewhere described himself as being unable to sleep (7:4) but suffering nightmares when he did sleep (7:14), as having severe halitosis (19:17) and being emaciated (19:20), and as having blackened, rotting skin and fevers (30:30). Scraping himself with a potsherd apparently relieved some of the itching associated with boils, and his sitting on ashes was an act of mourning (2:8).

Job's response to his second affliction is couched in terms of his refusal to heed his wife's suggestion that he curse God and die (2:9–10). We do not have enough information to enable us to evaluate her character. Her words could be read, at worst, as bitter rejection of God on her part or, at best, as compassion for Job and a desire to see his misery ended. What is important here is the fact that even the one nearest to Job could no longer see a reason for him to continue to patiently endure, but even against her counsel he remained devout. The focus of this text is not on the disposition of his wife but on the faithfulness of Job against all odds.

In 2:11–13, the text gives us the background for the dialogue between Job and his friends Eliphaz, Zophar, and Bildad.

Equally astonishing is the statement that they sat in silence and stared at him for a solid week (2:13)! On the other hand, we should not be surprised or skeptical about the fact that they came to "comfort" him. Their anger at Job and their castigation of him as a sinner only came about gradually. They initially came to relieve his pain and share his sorrow, as is indicated by their prolonged silence and weeping.

Geographical details are uncertain but seem to imply amazing distances. Teman or Tema, home of Eliphaz, may have been in Edom (Jer. 49:7, 20) or Arabia (Jer. 25:23). Shuah, the home of Bildad, seems to have been in Mesopotamia on the Euphrates. The region of Naamah is unknown; it is most certainly not the Naamah of Judah mentioned in Joshua 15:41.

- *Job suffered the most terrible fate any person*
- *could suffer. All his children died, all his pos-*
- *sessions were lost, and his health was broken*
- *in a most painful and pitiful manner. Never-*
- *theless, it was only because of his righteous-*
- *ness and not from any lack of character or*
- *spirituality that all this came upon him.*
- *From the earthly view, Job appears to be a*
- *sinner on whom God finally brought down*
- *judgment. From the heavenly view, he is seen*
- *to be the most saintly of men.*

QUESTIONS TO GUIDE YOUR STUDY

1. What is God's appraisal of Job?
2. Why does Satan doubt God's appraisal of Job?
3. What does God allow Satan to do?
4. What does Job's wife counsel him to do?

JOB'S OPENING SOLILOQUY (3:1–26)

Job's opening soliloquy is in three parts. The outline is as follows:

1. Cursing the day of his birth (3:2–16)
2. The grave a place of rest (3:17–26)
3. Job's current condition of unmitigated pain (3:23–26)

What may be lost on the casual reader is how Job reverses the language of creation in his lamentation. In contrast to God's decree, "Let there be light" (Gen. 1:3), Job calls for the day to be turned to darkness (vv. 3–6). Against God's creation of the stars (Gen. 1:16), Job wishes for the stars to go dark (v. 9). More than that, he calls for sorcerers to arouse "Leviathan," a monster representing death and chaos (v. 8). This calls to mind the initial chaos described in the creation account (Gen. 1:2). Job apparently wants Leviathan to devour the day of his birth, so sending the day back into a state of chaos or nothingness. The mention of Leviathan at this point cannot be accidental: The beast returns in a crucial role at the end of the book, as we shall see.

The day of birth is *for the individual* what creation is *for the whole world.* In cursing the day of his birth, Job rejects the work of God that brought the world and Job himself into existence. This explains why the three friends react with such astonishment and censure at Job's words in the following chapters. They understand that Job was saying that the world no longer made sense and that he could no longer endorse God's assessment that the world was "good" (Gen. 1:31). In calling for the world to end, or rather to have never begun, Job declares that his world has collapsed around him.

This is not just because Job was grieved by the loss of his children, his health, and his property. Job is not being petulant or indulging in self-pity. Rather, Job's "world" had collapsed in the sense that the belief structure or worldview that had sustained him seemed to have been proven wrong. Job enters the story with the same basic theology as the three friends, a theology teaching that God rewards and protects the righteous but pours out destruction upon the wicked. Throughout the speeches that follow, Job repeatedly declares that he is innocent of any wrongdoing, and thus that this calamity should not have befallen him. For Job, the world was no longer "good" and ought to be engulfed in darkness for precisely this reason: it has turned out that justice does not rule. A blameless man can be overwhelmed by calamities and end his days in bitter sorrow.

"Leviathan

Name of an ancient sea creature, literally means "coiled one."

To Job, it seems that all the teachings of the wise (such as are found in the book of Proverbs) have proven false. He comes to this conclusion not out of arrogance but simply because he knew that he was, as Job 1:1 tells us, entirely a righteous man. His friends will see the force of this and try to combat it in the only way they can—by asserting that Job is a sinner.

Job demonstrates his horror at how the world and his life have turned out by taking scenes that are normally beautiful and poignant and rejecting them as abhorrent. He wishes that the day on which they said, "It's a boy!" and his mother received him to her breasts would go into oblivion (vv. 3, 12). He wishes the joyful celebration of a new birth had never been heard (v. 7). In a world that no longer makes sense, normal celebration and joy are absurd.

Against the cruelty and absurdity of the world, Job looks upon the grave as a good thing. He claims that had he died at birth, he would now be in the same status as all the kings and mighty men of long ago (v. 14). Furthermore, he asserts that death represents deliverance to all whose lot was full of grief: the wicked, the weary, the prisoners, and the slaves (vv. 17–19). Death thus makes equals of kings, slaves, and the stillborn; it is, he implies, the closest thing to salvation one can find in this unjust world.

In his description of his wretched condition, Job makes two significant points. First, he says that he was a man whom God had "hedged in" (v. 23). This is noteworthy because it is precisely how Satan described God's treatment of Job (1:10). The difference, of course, is that Satan meant that God had set a wall of protection around Job, but Job meant that God imprisoned him. The different ways Job and Satan use the word *hedge* is an example of irony in Job. In due course, we will learn that both have misstated the work of God.

The second important comment at the end of Job's first speech is his outcry that the thing he dreaded has come upon him (v. 25). The foundation of Job's life has been the belief that God

Irony

A literary technique in which a text uses surprising and sometimes veiled contrasts for rhetorical purposes. A single word may be used in two contrasting ways in order to draw the reader into reflection. Or a character may make a statement that is true in a way the character does not realize.

would protect those who feared Him and that justice prevails in the world. His deepest fear and the worst thing that could happen to him was the discovery that his faith was misplaced. Now it seems that his hope has been proven hollow in the most dramatic and painfully possible manner.

- *Job desires that the day of his birth be swal-*
- *lowed in darkness because his world has*
- *fallen apart. In his despair, he considers*
- *death to be the only justice and bliss humans*
- *are likely to encounter.*

QUESTIONS TO GUIDE YOUR STUDY

1. What is the worst thing that happened to Job as a result of the disasters he experienced?
2. Describe how the use of "hedged in" is ironic.

ELIPHAZ'S FIRST RESPONSE (4:1–5:27)

Eliphaz's opening speech to Job is a model of tact and pastoral care. In subsequent responses, he and the other friends will become increasingly strident and condemnatory toward Job. At this point, however, Eliphaz is gentle and his response follows a simple outline:

    I. Job mildly rebuked (4:2–6)
    II. Justice still prevails (4:7–21)
       A. Proven by experience (4:7–11)
       B. Proven by personal revelation (4:12–21)
    III. Counsel for Job (5:1–27)
       A. Don't seek a mediator (5:1–7)
       B. Trust God (5:8–27)

Eliphaz first tempers his words by registering only mild surprise that Job would say such things. He reminds him that Job himself once gave counsel to the suffering and advised patience and faith; now Job is unable to practice what he had preached. Even so, Eliphaz affirms that Job was a man of piety (4:2–6).

The rhetorical question of 4:7, however, in a veiled way implies that Job must somehow deserve what has befallen him. If, as the question suggests, the upright do not suffer calamitous defeat, then one can only surmise that Job was not altogether upright. In fact, in Eliphaz's experience, it is those powerful people who "plow iniquity" whom God suddenly destroys. But who has been more powerful than Job? And upon whom has destruction fallen so suddenly?

But Eliphaz does not rely upon experience only as he makes his case to Job. He also claims that a revelation has come to him. His description seems to be an account of a prophetic experience; apparently such visions genuinely occurred in dreams or in visions of the night. For Eliphaz to claim that revelation supports his case is tantamount to a modern Christian citing the Bible to clench an argument. The spirit who glided past Eliphaz and made his hair stand on end declared that no created being, least of all a mortal, could be pure before God. The implied syllogism is: All beings are impure before God; Job is a created being; therefore, Job is impure before God. From this, one may draw the conclusion that God has every right to punish Job however He sees fit.

This begins what will be in the speeches of the friends a key premise of their argument. All people are corrupt; therefore, it is pointless for Job

The modern, Christian reader may well feel drawn to this line of thinking. After all, Romans 3:23 declares that all have sinned. The problem is that although the doctrine of universal depravity is valid, it expressly does not apply here! The text has already told us that Job was absolutely blameless (1:1), and it was because of his righteousness, not his sin, that he was suffering (1:6–12). Here and throughout the book, Job's three friends apply good theology to the wrong situation, and the result is their total inability to come to terms with Job's situation.

to contend that he is innocent and does not deserve what has befallen him.

In his counsel to Job, Eliphaz implies that there is no point to Job's seeking a heavenly intercessor, a "holy one," to plead his case (5:1). His point may be that the heavenly beings will not support Job's case; or it may be that even the angels cannot help him because they, too, are unclean before God (4:18). He goes on to describe the terrible fate of the wicked and pointedly mentions that their children suddenly perish (5:4), a grim—if covert—reminder of what has befallen Job's family.

Eliphaz's speech concludes with a beautiful exhortation to return to God, with assurances that God will deliver those who turn to Him and heal them of their afflictions (5:8–27). For all its beauty, however, it is entirely inappropriate. Eliphaz's counsel builds upon a central truth: "Blessed is the man whom God corrects" (5:17). In this case, however, God has not reproved Job at all. In addition, there are two ironies in Eliphaz's speech of which he is unaware. First, Eliphaz has preemptively scoffed at the idea of seeking a heavenly Intercessor, but Job, as he works through his dilemma, will build a compelling picture of the heavenly Redeemer/Intercessor, as we shall see. Second, Eliphaz assures Job that if he will commit himself to God, all will turn out well for him. This, in fact, will happen, but it happens in a way that Eliphaz does not expect and that condemns rather than vindicates Eliphaz and company (see 42:7).

JOB RESPONDS AND PRAYS (6:1–7:21)

In his response, Job again laments his situation and addresses both his companions and God. In outline form, his speech is as follows:

1. Job's first lament (6:2–13)
2. Job's disappointment in his friends (6:14–30)
3. Job's second lament (7:1–10)
4. Job's prayer (7:11–21)

In his first lament, Job declares that his pain is beyond his ability to bear, and this accounts for his harsh words (6:2–4). He then describes his predicament and response in a series of brief metaphors. First, he implies that animals do not bellow when they are satisfied (6:5), and second, he declares that he cannot eat insipid, tasteless food, such as an unsalted egg white (6:6). His meaning is that he, like a hungry animal, is bellowing in his pain but that he cannot be satisfied with the hollow, rehashed sayings of traditional theology (such as his three friends are giving). His pain goes beyond grieving over his losses; it includes the fact that no one can explain why this has happened to him. In this condition, Job despairs of ever finding relief from his sorrow and again expresses his feeling that he would be better off dead (6:8–13).

The translation of 6:14 is difficult, but probably one should follow the interpretation of several ancient versions and take it to mean, "Whoever deprives his friend of kindness forsakes the fear of the Almighty" (see NRSV). So saying, Job claims that his friends failed to give him the compassion a friend ought to give and so had brought down guilt on their own heads. He was as disappointed in them as thirsty travelers in a desert caravan who were disappointed when they arrived at the brook only to find it dried up (6:15–21). The metaphor implies that Job was famished for helpful words and he was not finding them. Job asserts that he had not sought something very difficult for them to provide,

White of an egg

The meaning of the Hebrew in 6:6 is uncertain. It may be that instead of the "white of an egg" it refers to the insipid juices of some plant indigenous to the region. Some translate it, "the juice of the mallows." Either way, it refers to some kind of tasteless food.

Sheol

The Hebrew word *Sheol*, which is often translated as the "grave" or as "Hades," is not so much a place as it is the condition of being dead. To the extent it is described at all, it is simply a place of darkness inhabited by shades. Christian readers should hesitate to read concepts of heaven or hell into Sheol, since the Old Testament texts that mention Sheol often do not deal with afterlife or last things.

such as money or protection from enemies; he only wanted honest, helpful answers. The friends responded with reproofs that missed the mark entirely because they did not apply to his situation (6:22–26). In a stinging remark, he compares them to a people who would gamble for possession of an orphan (6:27). If this seems unduly harsh, one should understand that Job, bereft of everything, considered himself like the orphan. His friends would rather throw Job away than honestly deal with what a severe blow his case was to their theology of reward and punishment.

In his second lament (7:1–10), Job bemoans the human condition of a life of unrelenting toil and sorrow, a condition that only ends in the darkness of Sheol. The slave longs for shade, and the laborer hopes for his wages: In short, human life is a wretched state of unfulfilled yearning in the midst of toil (7:2). Job himself represents this condition in its most pitiful form. Unable to endure his pain and sure that he did not have long to live, he describes himself as already caked in dirt and crawling with worms (7:5), a situation that obviously anticipates the grave.

■ *Eliphaz tactfully and respectfully exhorts*
■ *Job to repent; nevertheless, he also implies*
■ *that Job is in need of repentance. For all*
■ *their beauty, his words are inappropriate*
■ *or will be fulfilled in a way that Eliphaz*
■ *does not expect. Job responds by asking*
■ *both his friends and God to show him spe-*
■ *cifically what he has done to deserve his*
■ *afflictions.*

QUESTIONS TO GUIDE YOUR STUDY

1. How does Eliphaz diagnose Job's situation?
2. What does Eliphaz counsel Job to do?
3. What is Sheol?

BILDAD'S FIRST RESPONSE (8:1–22)

Bildad is a step down from Eliphaz. He parrots orthodox teachings about how God punishes the wicked but protects the upright while at the same time showing the most cruel insensitivity to what has befallen Job. "If your children sinned against him, he delivered them into the power of their transgression," he blurted out in verse 4. These are hardly the words to say to a man whose children have all just died in a terrible calamity, especially when there is no evidence that they had done anything wrong.

Bildad is a champion of the *theology of retribution*. The essential teaching of this theology is that God rewards the upright and punishes the wicked. The rewards generally include a long life, many children, prosperity, and health; and the penalties are the loss of the same.

For Bildad, it was enough that teachers of the former generations embraced the theology of retribution (vv. 8–10). He is nothing if not a traditionalist! Those who reject this theology, he contended, build lives that are as fragile as a spider's web (vv. 14–15). It is important to recognize that what Bildad affirmed is not wrong; it is simply unsuitable here.

JOB RESPONDS AND PRAYS AGAIN (9:1–10:22)

Job appears to ignore Bildad entirely in his answer; he focuses on the sovereignty of God, whereas Bildad devoted his speech to an assertion that God condemns the guilty and saves the

This theology is not necessarily wrong; one finds it everywhere in the book of Proverbs. It becomes dangerous, however, if one exaggerates it or uses it as a tool for judging others. The theology of retribution is foundational to biblical wisdom, and mastery of it represents the first step toward maturity. Books such as Job and Ecclesiastes, however, go beyond this theology to engage more complex issues of life.

Rahab

In 9:13, Job even asserts that the *subordinates of Rahab* crouch before God. "Rahab" in this context is not the woman of the book of Joshua. Rather, it is a dragon of the sea and a monster of chaos (Ps. 89:10). In some texts, "Rahab" is a byname for Egypt, the great enemy of Israel (Ps. 87:4), but Job does not here speak of Egypt. For Job, the expression "subordinates of Rahab" is functionally equivalent to the English phrase, "the hounds of hell." He means that even the monsters of the abyss do God's bidding, so naturally Job has no chance of resisting him. Rahab is sometimes identified with Leviathan, the great beast of Job 41. In that text, God will also describe how He controls Rahab/Leviathan. Here, the very idea fills Job with terror; in Job 41, it will bring him to repentance.

innocent. In fact, Job does respond to the previous speech. Bildad's point was simply, "God judges fairly," and Job's answer is, "God does whatever He wants to." In short, Job argues that God is arbitrary. The outline of this speech is:

1. God is irresistible and incontestable (9:2–35)
2. Job's prayer (10:1–22)

If there is one element of Job's faith that is unshaken, it is this: he has no doubt about the sovereignty and power of God. In 9:2–13, Job eloquently gives expression to the enormity of God's strength. He moves mountains, shakes the earth, darkens the sky, and rules the constellations. Nevertheless, there is no joy or celebration in Job's words. God's power is not for him a reason for comfort but for terror. The examples Job cites of God's omnipotence are for the most part violent or horrifying, such as a great earthquake (9:5–6). Thus, Job does not cling to God but cringes before Him (9:3, 11–13).

In 9:14–20, Job declares that God's irresistible power eliminates any hope that Job might stand before God and get a fair hearing. Why should the Almighty listen to puny Job? The problem with Job's reasoning is not that he is wrong about the magnitude of God's power. Because Job cannot comprehend any purpose or reason behind God's actions, he assumes that God's behavior makes no sense. Job is correct about God's sovereignty, and he is correct to maintain his innocence in the face of his friends' accusations, but he is wrong to portray God as arbitrary. Interestingly, the other speakers, vexed at their inability to silence his claims of innocence, will soon defend God's justice by appealing to God's authority in a manner very similar to what Job has just done (e.g., 35:1–16). That is, they too, will almost speak of God as arbitrary, but they will present this as a good thing!

In this condition, Job despairs completely of ever getting justice from God (9:14–31). Even if he is completely clean, God will push him in the mud (that is, treat him as if he were guilty, 9:30–31)! As a good, Old Testament monotheist, Job does not draw back from affirming the rule of God over all situations, even over cases where the rich steal land from the poor (9:24). But does not this very fact prove that God allows injustice to thrive?

In the midst of his despair, Job opens the subject of the intercessor or referee, a figure that will become an important subtheme in his speeches (9:33–35). Here, he only expresses the forlorn wish that there were a third party, a figure who could stand in the middle ground between a man and God and bring peace. In subsequent speeches, the intercessor will occupy a much more significant place, and Job will adopt an attitude that is more characterized by faith than hopelessness.

In 10:1, Job has something of a change of mind. Before, he felt it was hopeless even to try to make any arguments before God (9:15). Here, he says that since his cause is lost anyway, he might as well state his case.

In the prayer of 10:2–22, Job's tone is alternately pleading and sarcastic. We should not take the harsh tone of some of his words as an indication of impiety, however. Many of the prayers and declarations of Old Testament saints are to Western readers surprisingly bold in their mode of addressing God. In Psalm 42:9, the psalmist asks God why He has forgotten His unhappy servant. Similarly, in Psalm 44:23, the people

27

ask God why He has fallen asleep while their enemies destroy them. Psalm 88 is almost a model for blunt praying. But no one could say that these prayers are irreverent or unworthy, and we should hesitate to condemn Job here.

In addition, the challenging rhetorical questions of 10:4–5 ("Do you have eyes of flesh? Do you see as people see? Are your days like the days of mortals, or your years like the years of a man?") are more than an angry retort to God. Those words implicitly look for the intercessor of 9:33. Job believes that God has no concept of what it is like to be human. We are limited in our ability to comprehend what happens to us ("eyes of flesh") and unable to withstand the blows that God reigns down on us ("days of mortals"). If only God could somehow share in this limitation, He would know what it is to be human and become more compassionate, Job implies. For the book of Hebrews, Job's yearning is not an idle fancy; it gives expression to a necessary component in bringing about reconciliation between God and humanity: a divine-human intermediary. Jesus, although the Son of God, was made for a little while lower than the angels, took on human flesh, and participated in human weakness. It was in that very condition that He destroyed the works of the devil (which as we shall see is another idea of great significance in the book of Job). Having been one of us, the Son of God is not ashamed to call us His family but serves as a faithful high priest making intercession in our behalf (Heb. 2:9–18).

"Therefore, He had to be made like His brethren in all things, that He might become a merciful and faithful high priest in things pertaining to God, to make propitiation for the sins of the people" (Heb. 2:17, NASB).

In 10:8–12, Job pleads with God to be compassionate on the grounds that God is his maker. God should care for His own. Instead, it seems that the only reason God made Job was so that He could find fault with him and crush him

(10:13–17). If that is why God put people on earth, so that He could try them and find them wanting, Job wishes (again) that he had never been born in the first place (10:18–19). After all, he did not choose to come into this world. After a life of suffering under the scrutiny of a disapproving deity, moreover, mortals make their way to the murky chaos of Sheol (10:20–22). At this point, Job's view of the human condition could almost be put on a bumper sticker: "Life: first you're born, then you get punished for all your sins, then you die."

■ *Bildad advances a theology of retribution to*
■ *explain what has happened to Job. Job*
■ *acknowledges that God has great power, but*
■ *this power is a terror rather than a reason to*
■ *celebrate. In his despondency, Job begs God*
■ *to show some mercy. Nevertheless, Job also*
■ *introduces the idea of the intercessor, some-*
■ *one to bring God and man together.*

QUESTIONS TO GUIDE YOUR STUDY

1. Briefly describe and evaluate Bildad's understanding of God.

2. What attributes of God seem most real to Job at this time?

3. In what other Old Testament writings are emotions expressed as they are in Job?

ZOPHAR'S FIRST RESPONSE (11:1–20)

Eliphaz was tactful but firm; Bildad was tactless, but Zophar is simply angry. He makes no effort to assuage Job's anger; he instead, makes a frontal assault upon him. Nevertheless, his words

Zophar accuses Job of being an idle talker and a mocker (vv. 2–3). These are not trivial insults. In Proverbs, mockery and empty speech are the marks of a fool, a person who is reprobate and opposed to all that is right. Fools love mockery (Prov. 1:22) and in particular mock at making amends for their sins (Prov. 14:9). They are insolent and hateful to those who rebuke them (Prov. 9:7–8), and they never listen to sound advice (Prov. 13:1). Above all, they are proud and arrogant (Prov. 21:24). As far as Zophar is concerned, Job is all of these.

are really very similar to those of the other friends. The outline of this speech is:

1. Direct rebuke of Job (11:2–6)
2. The mysteries of God (11:7–12)
3. Demand for repentance (11:13–20)

Thus, Zophar is outraged at Job's claims of innocence (v. 4), even though the reader knows that Job is right. He wants nothing so much as for God to come down and confront Job with a catalog of all of the offenses by which Job has earned every blow he received (vv. 5–6). The irony here is that God will come and confront Job, but He will not accuse Job of anything at all except for being brash in demanding a chance to confront God face-to-face. Instead, God will demand that Zophar bring an offering to atone for his own sin!

In verses 7–12, Zophar anticipates Elihu's speech and to some degree even God's speech by asserting that God's wisdom and power are beyond Job's comprehension. The problem here is not that what Zophar says about the grandeur of God is wrong; it is that Zophar himself does not really understand how God's rule over the universe relates to Job's case. As far as Zophar is concerned, the only point is that God is powerful and can do whatever He wants. God Himself will explain the real meaning of His sovereignty in His speech.

Zophar throws Job's words back in his face in verse 12. Job had explained his outburst by saying that a wild donkey only brays when it is hungry (6:5). Zophar considers the analogy to a wild donkey to be particularly appropriate for Job; he is a stupid, stubborn man!

Zophar closes with yet another appeal for Job to repent of whatever sins he had committed that brought about all this calamity (vv. 13–20). When he exhorts Job to put away the sin that is in his hand (v. 14), he is saying that he is sure Job is hiding something. There is, again, nothing particularly wrong with the theology of Zophar's speech, but it is irrelevant because Job has nothing to repent from. Furthermore, Zophar holds to a particularly inflexible doctrine of retribution. The wicked perish and the righteous are happy, he thinks. His theology has difficulty comprehending the idea of the suffering servant of God.

■ *Zophar considers Job to be an arrogant,*
■ *self-righteous mocker of the truth. He thinks*
■ *Job has no grasp of the magnitude of God's*
■ *power and wishes God would appear and*
■ *rebuke Job. Certain that Job is also hiding*
■ *some sins, Zophar urges him to repent.*

QUESTIONS TO GUIDE YOUR STUDY

1. What is Zophar's approach to Job?

2. How does Zophar view God's wisdom?

3. What does Zophar counsel Job to do?

JOB OPENS THE SECOND CYCLE (12:1–14:22)

Job begins the second cycle of debate with what is possibly the finest insult in literature: "No doubt you are a people and wisdom will die with you!" That is, he sarcastically says that his three friends constitute a class of people unto themselves, "the wise," and that with their deaths wisdom itself will vanish from the face of the earth. With this, Job begins another discourse that moves into a prayer, as follows:

1. Job's wisdom is no less than that of the friends (12:2–13:12)
2. Job will take his case to God (13:13–17)
3. Job's prayer and case against God (13:18–14:22)

Job opens with a protest that they do him wrong in treating him like a fool who is untaught in the ways of wisdom. Once he was renowned for piety and sagacity; now they mock him by tutoring him in rudimentary doctrine (12:3–4). The translation of 12:5 is much disputed, but a good case can be made for the NKJV interpretation, "A lamp is despised in the thought of one who is at ease; *It is* made ready for those whose feet slip." If this interpretation is right, then Job himself is the lamp whom people of power smiled at condescendingly even though he gave direction to those who stumbled. Now, however, everyone mocks Job. In 12:6, Job describes a world in chaos; thieves and blasphemers live securely (while Job himself is in ruins). The realities of the world have made a mockery of the "wisdom" that Job once espoused.

In the tradition of the sages, Job tells his friends to go and learn from the animals (12:7–12; see Prov. 30:24–31). Here, however, suggestion has a barb to it. Job had called them a "people," the class of learned men (12:2). But these learned men cannot see what is so obvious to the birds, animals, fish, and even plants: Life is inherently insecure, and God holds all in His hands. Once again for Job this idea no longer gives comfort but only dread. Our well-being hangs on a thread, and God might drop that thread at any moment.

Job describes the work of God in 12:13–25. As before, Job has no doubt about God's power, but that power is very unsettling. He is the God of upheavals. Throughout this text, God keeps the human race in a state of disorder and uncertainty. Counselors, kings, and priests are overthrown; and fools take their places. Nations rise and fall. No one is safe, and nothing is secure. But it is not merely the fact that the world is an unstable place; God is bringing about the instability. As far as Job can see, God's activity has neither reason nor goal. Chaos is simply the order of the day. God will address this issue in His speech and bring Job to a clearer understanding of what God is actually doing.

Job renews his claim to be no less instructed in orthodox theology than are his friends, but he adds to this a more direct attack on them (13:1–12). Job fully understands the situation. The traditional theology of retribution has failed, and no one can give Job a good reason not to think that God is arbitrary and unfair. The only solution is for Job to take his questions to God Himself (13:1–3). But the three friends refuse to face facts. Desiring to uphold traditional theology, they whitewash the ugly truth with lies, give medicine that does not heal, and offer proverbs of ashes and arguments of clay. Unable to give any help, the wisest thing they could do would be to shut up! In one of the most jolting lines of the book, Job says that they speak lies for God (13:7).

In 14:13–17, Job prepares to take his stand before God and make his arguments. In a culture where even seeing God was thought to be fatal (Judg. 13:22), Job understood that the action he was taking was suicidal. He was not going to "curse God and die," but he would face God. At the same time, he felt that he would be vindicated in that he at least courageously held

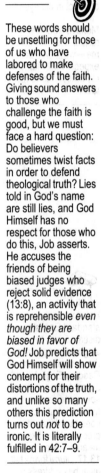

These words should be unsettling for those of us who have labored to make defenses of the faith. Giving sound answers to those who challenge the faith is good, but we must face a hard question: Do believers sometimes twist facts in order to defend theological truth? Lies told in God's name are still lies, and God Himself has no respect for those who do this, Job asserts. He accuses the friends of being biased judges who reject solid evidence (13:8), an activity that is reprehensible *even though they are biased in favor of God!* Job predicts that God Himself will show contempt for their distortions of the truth, and unlike so many others this prediction turns out *not* to be ironic. It is literally fulfilled in 42:7–9.

"Though he slay me"

The Jerusalem Bible renders 13:15 as, "Let him kill me if he will; I have not other hope than to justify my conduct in his eyes."

Moffat's translation reads: "He may kill me—what else can I expect? I will maintain my innocence to his face."

to the truth. The traditional translation of 13:15, "Though he slay me, yet will I trust in him," although stirring to read, is probably not correct. The Hebrew should more accurately be rendered, "He is about to slay me; I have no hope. But I will argue my ways before Him." Job is about to pray, but it will be a very unusual prayer: it will be a prayer in which he lays out his case against God.

When Job declares that he will argue his "ways" before God (13:15), he means that he will defend his integrity, his beliefs, and his refusal to accept that what has happened to him is just.

In verses 18–19, Job issues a formal challenge to God that was perhaps similar to how a man would initiate a lawsuit against another party in court. It might be translated like this: "Look now, I am setting forth my case; and I know that I will win. Who is this who contends against me? If I kept silent, I would die." In other words, he is so certain of the justice of his case that he cannot contain himself.

Hebrew, unlike standard English, distinguishes the singular and plural of the second person. Reading English, we do not know whether *you* is one person or a hundred, but Hebrew uses two different pronouns to make the meaning clear. In 13:17, *plural* forms tell us Job is addressing the friends, but in 13:19–20, *singular* forms tell us that he is talking to God.

Job presses his case in the words that follow. First, he asks that God give him a fair hearing and not simply crush Job like some bug. He is willing to let God speak first or respond to his complaints (13:20–22). He wishes that God would quit shaking and terrifying him and would simply listen and answer (13:23–27). In 13:26, Job is not confessing to having lived a riotous youth; he means that God is so desperate to find something to punish Job for that He is reaching back into Job's childhood.

Job opens his case by describing how God has made humans (13:28–14:22). In short, God made us weak and mortal. We waste away like moth-eaten rags (13:28) and live for a terribly brief span of years (14:1). What is the point in God's bringing down judgment on such ephemeral creatures (14:3)? You made us from the dirt, he contends, do You expect to find purity in us (14:4)? At least let us live our few days in peace (14:5–6).

We humans truly have a miserable lot (14:7–12). Even trees have some hope of sending up new shoots and living again after they have been felled, but no such prospect appears for people. We simply die and vanish away, like the water of a dried river.

Suddenly, it seems that another revelatory lightning bolt falls upon Job. Perhaps the salvation of humans is in the resurrection (14:13–17). God could call us back from the grave, redeem us from corruption, and put an end to sin and judgment. At the moment, this hope is only a thin, desperate prayer on Job's lips; but like the wish for an intercessor, it expresses an essential aspect of salvation and reconciliation with God. Death must be overcome. Mortality must be swallowed in victory. Corruption must die, but people must live again in purity before God. Without resurrection, we have no hope (1 Cor. 15:16–19).

But Job turns away from this lofty desire and returns to humans as they really are, as far as he can tell. Just as surely as the waters erode the soil, so human life slips away (14:18–22). The metaphor is particularly apt. Just as eroded soil dissipates, then is lost forever, and no longer good for anything, so human life disintegrates before our eyes.

■ *Job no longer has any use for the words of his*
■ *friends. He already knows everything they*
■ *want to say, and he is tired of being treated*
■ *like a schoolboy. He will cast his own life to*
■ *the winds and take his case to God. Before*
■ *God, he declares that God made humans as*
■ *frail creatures and ought to at least give them*
■ *a little peace in this life. But in a moment of*
■ *profound insight, Job discovers that the real*
■ *salvation for humanity is in the resurrection.*

QUESTIONS TO GUIDE YOUR STUDY

1. What does Job tell his counselors will happen to their wisdom?

2. Why does Job encourage his counselors to consult the animals and learn from them?

3. What does Job most want from God?

ELIPHAZ'S SECOND RESPONSE (15:1–35)

Job clearly has not finished making his case before God, and anyway, he does not want to hear any more from his friends. But Eliphaz can take no more of this "blasphemy" and interrupts Job's address to God. Incensed, he bellows out a thunderous discourse on the fate of the wicked. The outline of his speech is as follows:

1. Job's arrogance (15:2–13)

2. The ruination of the wicked (15:14–35)

Stung by Job's sarcastic remark that the three friends were last of the wise men on earth (12:2), Eliphaz repays him in kind. He accuses Job of being a windbag who spews forth worthless, foolish words (15:2–3). Worse yet, Job is saying things that undermine devotion to God

(v. 4). Job has joined the ranks of sophisticated evildoers. In modern terms, as far as Eliphaz is concerned, Job has become a sneering atheist! Above all, it is pure arrogance for Job to think he understands the situation better than they. He is but one man, but the wisdom of the ages is on the side of Eliphaz and his friends (vv. 7–10). Eliphaz refuses to consider the possibility that Job's complaints against traditional thinking do not spring from pride or from a crafty dismantling of wise teachings; they come instead from his own experience and a willingness to face brute facts. For Eliphaz, Job has become incomprehensibly irreverent (vv. 11–13).

Eliphaz repeats the argument of 4:17–19, that even angels are not pure before God and that people, evil people in particular, are much more vile in God's eyes (vv. 14–16). He reiterates, too, that his teachings represent the consensus of the elders (vv. 17–19). He stresses the purity of the tradition he espouses when he declares that it comes from a time when no aliens passed through the land (v. 19). It is not clear what time or place he is referring to, but the idea is that pure wisdom is undefiled by foreign ideas.

The aged Eliphaz maintains the traditional view that aged people understand the world better than do young people and that old teachings are better than new ideas. While this perspective has validity (see Prov. 4:1–5), it should not be elevated to the status of absolute truth.

Eliphaz then gives an extended portrait of the suffering of the wicked, and it is impossible to doubt that he is using Job himself as a case in point. The wicked are filled with terror (vv. 20–21; see 6:4), plundered by marauders (v. 21; see 1:13–19), plunged into darkness and at death's door (vv. 22–23; see 10:21–22), and yet shaking their fists angrily at God (vv. 25–26). The wicked wander in a wasteland (vv. 23, 28; see 12:24). Their riches, in which they trust, will disappear (vv. 27–29; see 1:10–11). Eliphaz did no less than to take everything that had happened to Job and everything he had said and shape it into a portrait of a wicked man getting what he deserves. When he says that the wicked are like vines that are stripped of unripe grapes (v. 33), he is asserting that their children die young, a point that is especially cruel when directed at Job (see 1:18–19). This is, of course, grossly unfair to Job, but Eliphaz only treated Job's protests as more proof of his guilt.

- *Eliphaz, enraged at Job's remarks, interrupts*
- *him and paints a picture of the downfall of*
- *the wicked that is largely drawn from Job's*
- *own words and experiences.*

JOB LAMENTS AND PRAYS (16:1–17:16)

In this text, Job gives way to his frustration, confusion, and anger in a way that at first appears to be rambling and almost incoherent. But he has given his speech a carefully constructed structure known as chiasmus. This structure shows that this is not just an emotional outburst. More importantly, a confession of faith stands at the very center of the whole (16:18-21). In a chiasmus, the central element is often the most important part of all. The structure of the text is as follows:

Chiasmus

A way of arranging a text so that the second half parallels the first half but does it in reverse order. For example, if the first half has three parts A, B, and C, the second half will have three parallel parts in reverse order: C, B, and A. A single verse or an entire chapter can be arranged as a chiasmus.

A Complaint against the friends and lament (16:1–5)

    B Prayer and complaint to God (16:6–14)

        C Lament (16:15-17)

            D Confession of faith (16:18–21)

        C Lament (16:22–17:2)

    B Prayer and complaint to God (17:3–9)

A Complaint against the friends and lament (17:10–16).

Job sends Eliphaz's insults back upon his own head: I am not the windbag, you are (16:2–3; see 15:2–3)! But he does not simply rail against them; he also appeals to their sense of decency. He asserts that if their places were reversed, he would not piously condemn them as they have done to him; he would instead seek to give them encouragement and comfort (16:4–5).

Job abruptly turns away from his friends and addresses what is now his only concern, his case against God (16:6–14). The Hebrew indicates that he rapidly moves between speaking about God (third person) and speaking to God (second person), although some translations do not show this. Job says he might as well speak his mind; whether vocal or silent, he is still in agony (16:6). When Job says that God has destroyed his whole "company" (16:7), he apparently is referring to his household. Job uses a series of metaphors that are astoundingly violent to make his case: God has come upon Job as a wild beast bearing claws and teeth (16:9) and has attacked him like a warrior who commands his troops to fire arrows at their enemy (16:12–14). Although the images are harsh, they are not unusual in the Old Testament. In Hosea, for example, God describes Himself in similar terms (Hos. 13:7–8).

In 16:15–17, Job laments his current condition. He has all the characteristics of a broken sinner (wearing sackcloth, bowed down in the dust, weeping) even though he is entirely innocent.

In the midst of this sorrow, Job again turns to the theme of the heavenly intercessor (16:18–21). He asks the earth not to hide his blood that has been wrongfully shed (v. 18), because to hide it would be to conceal an injustice forever. But

"So I will be like a lion to them;
Like a leopard I will lie in wait by the wayside.
I will encounter them like a bear robbed of her cubs,
And I will tear open their chests;
There I will also devour them like a lioness,
As a wild beast would tear them"
(Hos. 13:7–8, NASB).

more importantly, Job declares his belief that he actually has an advocate in heaven. Verses 19–21 are difficult in Hebrew, but a reasonable translation would be: "Even now my witness is in heaven. My advocate is on high. My friends should be my intercessors while my eye weeps toward God, and he will arbitrate for a man with God just as though it were between one mortal and another." Job is saying that although all his friends have turned against him, he is sure the heavenly advocate will intercede for him.

Job does not tell us anything about this advocate. Is he an angel, or God Himself? Nowhere in the Bible do angels have this role. Could Job have imagined that God could somehow play both the role of judge and defense advocate? What is only obscurity in the book of Job becomes the amazing work of salvation in the New Testament. Paul could boast that what Job dimly saw in the distance is now a glorious reality.

"Who is to condemn? It is Christ Jesus who died, yes, who was raised, who is at the right hand of God, who indeed intercedes for us" (Rom. 8:34, NRSV).

Job falls back into lamentation in 16:22–17:2. He sees himself ready to die in the most wretched of conditions with "mockers" (his friends) all around him.

He resumes praying in 17:3–9. His complaints here, however, are not directed against God but against his friends; in fact, he asks for God's help against the three friends. His request that God provide collateral for him (17:3) is mysterious, but the meaning is revealed in Psalm 119:122, where the psalmist petitions God, "Ensure your servant's well-being; let not the arrogant oppress me." That is, Job was asking God to vindicate him in the face of the condemnation his friends had laid on him. He protested that God had blinded their eyes to the truth (17:4) and asserted that failure to show loyalty to one's friend is a grievous sin (17:5). Nevertheless, Job still suffers under the hand of God; no sign of vindication seems near (17:6–9).

Concluding his speech, Job declared that not one of his friends had any sense (17:10). The reason for this harsh verdict is that they continually urged him to repent and hope in God, saying that if he did so God would deliver him from all troubles. But it was God who afflicted Job to begin with, and he has nothing from which to repent. God has brought him to death's door, and he is sure the end is near (17:11–16). Thus, their words are meaningless to him.

■ *Job is dismayed at his friends' refusal to give*
■ *him any comfort, and he is despondent that*
■ *God has brought him to this condition. Nev-*
■ *ertheless, he has hope for a heavenly inter-*
■ *cessor to plead his case.*

QUESTIONS TO GUIDE YOUR STUDY

1. What criticism does Eliphaz direct toward Job?
2. What does Eliphaz see as being the destiny of the wicked?
3. What does Job most want to do at this point?

BILDAD'S SECOND RESPONSE (18:1–21)

Bildad responds to Job with what is little more than an extended description of the fate of the wicked. The speech is in two parts:

1. Reproaches against Job (18:2–4)
2. The destruction of the wicked (5–21)

The Hebrew of 18:2–3 is unusual since Bildad uses the plural forms of "you" and "your," as though he were talking to more than one person.

Bildad perhaps uses the plural for *you* and *your* to indicate that Job is a member of a group, the mockers, who exasperate the godly with their impious words. In addition, the meaning of the Hebrew is quite obscure here. The beginning of verse 2 could mean, "How long until (people like) you make an end to words?" But it probably means, "How long will (people like) you lay verbal traps?" It is clear, at any rate, that Bildad has no more patience for any more of Job's wrangling. He wonders if Job wants the whole moral structure of the universe to be changed to suit him (v. 4).

Bildad insists that the wicked are punished and that this proves that God is governing the world rightly (vv. 5–21). His discourse is nicely crafted and appealing, but we have to wonder what we are to make of it.

Is Bildad right? Are the wicked punished as he says they are? In one sense, Bildad is right. Ultimately, God will triumph over evil; and every wrong will be righted. All the wicked face judgment and destruction.

Bildad is refusing to see the reality that Job has clearly described, and he even condemns Job for seeing that reality. In this world, there is a great deal of injustice; and often it seems as though the wicked do escape punishment. Furthermore, the righteous sometimes suffer grievously. These are the facts that Job is facing. Bildad does not have the profound vision of faith that sees the ultimate victory of God even in the dark days when evil seems to have won; he simply declines to open his eyes, lest he should see disturbing sights.

Like the other friends, Bildad also jabs at Job with painful barbs. He declares that none of the offspring of the wicked survive (v. 19) and that men from the east and west are appalled at how far the wicked fall (v. 20). It would not be lost on Job that his children were all dead and that three friends have come from afar to look in horror upon him.

■ *Bildad insists that the wicked are simply*
■ *destroyed and that everyone can see that it is*
■ *so. For him, this proves that Job is wrong in*
■ *what he says and guilty of sin, too.*

JOB PLEADS AND MOURNS BUT HOPES (19:1–29)

In this text, appeals and warnings to the friends provide the framework for the entire speech. Job's agony over the treatment he has received from his friends reaches a crescendo, but at the same time, so does his faith in the heavenly redeemer. His speech has the following outline:

1. A plea to the friends (19:2–4)
2. God has deprived Job of justice (19:5–12)
3. God has turned everyone against Job (19:13–20)
4. A second plea to the friends (19:21–22)
5. The heavenly redeemer (19:23–27)
6. A warning to the friends (19:28–29)

Job begs his friends to stop accusing him of wickedness (vv. 2–4). Their words are untrue, but they are harsh, and they hurt. In despair, Job asks them what business it is of theirs if he is in the wrong; it is his affair (v. 4). This does not mean that a friend should never rebuke a friend. To the contrary, biblical wisdom considers this to be a duty (Prov. 28:23). Nevertheless, honest rebukes are redemptive, patient, and discerning. Job's friends have condemned Job mercilessly not because they knew of any particular offenses he had committed but because they

Ten times

Job tells his friends that they have verbally assaulted him "ten times" (19:2). This is simply a round number that means "many times." One should not seek for ten specific reproaches against Job. Another example of this use of the number ten is in Genesis 31:7.

were afraid to face the consequences of admitting that so much calamity had befallen a good person.

The whole of 19:5–12 can be summarized as follows: "If you think that my condition is proof that I am a sinner, you should step back and recognize that God has made me suffer without just cause. My troubles are no proof of guilt." Job reinforces this portrayal of injustice with a series of metaphors. God is a hunter who has caught Job in a net (v. 6). God is like an indifferent passerby who takes no notice when Job is assaulted and calls for help (v. 7). God is like a man who blocks paths in the wilderness, forcing the traveler off the path and into the wilderness (v. 8). This metaphor is especially telling; it implies that Job was walking in the right way until God Himself forced him out of it. Now Job does not know where the right way is. God has stripped Job, uprooted him, set a fire against him, and ordered His troops to attack him (vv. 9–12).

More pitiful yet, God has turned all of Job's loved ones and acquaintances against him (19:13–20). Job describes three types of people who have turned against him. First are the "servants," people who had been Job's subordinates but now show contempt for him. Second are the "guests," those who have received kindness from Job but now do not repay him with kindness. Third are the "relatives" and "friends," those with whom Job thought he shared mutual love but who now abandon him. In short, everyone he thought he could turn to has scorned him. The line translated, "I have escaped by the skin of my teeth" (v. 20, NRSV), although it has been adopted into the English language, is very obscure in Hebrew. No one knows what it really means; "escape" does not fit the context.

When Job says that his breath was loathsome to his wife (v. 17), the literal meaning is not the main point. Although it was probably the case that his diseased condition gave him foul breath, the point here is what foul breath represents. Job's meaning is that his wife finds him repulsive.

It is not surprising that Job would feel a need for pity (vv. 21–22). But it is this very despondency that causes Job to turn away from his friends and seek comfort in the heavenly redeemer (vv. 25–27). It is ironic that Job should wish that his words were written down in a book since we are reading those words in a book (vv. 23–24). The reason for this desire is that he believed that future generations would weigh his words objectively and they would recognize that he was in the right.

Job sees the heavenly redeemer as a savior who will appear at the end of the age as the culmination of the plan of God to bring salvation. Job assumes that he will soon die and that people will throw out his body like garbage. Nevertheless, in the resurrection, he will see God (or the heavenly redeemer) from his own eyes and recognize Him not as an enemy—as He is now—but as a friend.

Job's vision of hope has reached its climax. He began with a tentative, almost wistful yearning for a heavenly intercessor to stand between himself and God (9:33–35). He then added to this the assertion that the salvation of people demands resurrection (14:13–17). After this, he wished again for a heavenly intercessor to take up his case where his friends have failed him

The Hebrew of verses 25–27 is a little obscure. A possible rendition is: "I know that my Redeemer lives and that the Final One will rise over the dust. After they have done away with my skin, from my flesh I shall have a vision of God. I will have this vision myself; my eyes will see that He is no enemy. My heart yearns within me!" The Hebrew word here translated "the Final One" (often translated here as "at the last") appears in Isaiah 44:6 and 48:12 where God says, "I am the first and the last."

(16:18–21). Here, he draws it all together into a grand vision of the redeemer who will arise "over the dust" in the end times. The dust, in Job, represents human mortality, corruption, and frailty, just as in Genesis 3 God had told Adam that he was of the dust and would return to it. The heavenly redeemer triumphs over death and the grave and brings the gift of resurrection to His people. Job declares that after his dead body has been disposed of he will yet see God with his eyes, an expectation that plainly describes resurrection. He knows that in that day God will no longer terrify him. He looks for the day described in Revelation 21:3–4, when God will dwell with His people and wipe away their tears, and they will no longer fear death.

Encouraged by this vision, Job turns from pleading with his friends and gives them a warning: In the end, there will be a just judgment, and the friends had better watch their words lest they fall into condemnation (vv. 28–29). Their expression "the root of the matter is found in him" (v. 28, NRSV) means, "The source of all this trouble is Job's sin." Job is certain that somehow he will be vindicated.

"And I heard a loud voice from the throne, saying, 'Behold, the tabernacle of God is among men, and He shall dwell among them, and they shall be His people, and God Himself shall be among them, and He shall wipe away every tear from their eyes; and there shall no longer be any death; there shall no longer be any mourning, or crying, or pain; the first things have passed away'" (Rev. 21:3–4, NASB).

- *The cruel condemnation Job had received has*
- *driven him to distraction. He pleads for com-*
- *passion and laments how all have turned*
- *against him. In the midst of this grief, how-*
- *ever, he returns to the idea of the heavenly*
- *redeemer and the resurrection. Job affirms*
- *his hope that this redeemer will raise him up*
- *so that he will see God.*

QUESTIONS TO GUIDE YOUR STUDY

1. In Bildad's view, is it possible for a person to suffer and not deserve it?
2. What does Job now ask of his friends?
3. What is the source of Job's hope?

ZOPHAR'S SECOND RESPONSE (20:1–29)

It is odd that Zophar does not interact at all with Job's confession of faith in a heavenly redeemer. It is as though he did not hear it or could not comprehend it. It seems that the only thing Zophar has grasped is: Job is claiming that he did not deserve to be punished and that he is scorning the wisdom of the three friends. Zophar claims to feel insulted (v. 3), and he wants to set matters right. He thus plunges into yet another speech on how severely God punishes the wicked. The outline is as follows:

1. Zophar's outrage (20:2–3)
2. The punishment of the wicked (20:4–29)

Once again one of the friends declares how terribly the wicked suffer, and once again he obviously has Job in mind as a case in point. The wicked may for a time be high and mighty, but they will collapse to the earth (as did Job). Verse 11 says that their children, who were once young and vigorous, will die with them (as did Job's children). Zophar asserts that such people hide wickedness under their tongues because sin is sweet to them (v. 12). To Job, his point appears to be that he is sure Job is harboring some secret iniquity. Zophar argues that God will force the wicked to give up what they have seized (vv. 13, 15).

The fact that Zophar is unjustly hostile to God should not blind us to the fact that much of what he says is accurate and compelling. He portrays the wicked as greedily holding on to

Verse 16 is unusual. It literally says, "He will suck the poison of cobras; the tongue of a snake will slay him." This is a peculiar way to describe being bitten by a snake. It may be that Zophar is saying that the wicked participate in their own demise by voluntarily giving themselves to the serpent. The tongue of the snake naturally recalls the speaking snake, the embodiment of evil, in Genesis 3.

In 20:27, Zophar says that the heavens and earth will testify against Job. This means that the natural order is offended at his effrontery in challenging God. Similar language is found in Isaiah 1:2.

everything they can get although this greed is their downfall. They have no peace; they cannot rest if some prize escapes them (v. 20). They consume extravagantly and cannot save for the future (v. 21). They will lose what they have acquired, and God will require satisfaction for all their sins (vv. 15, 18).

Zophar's description of the wrath of God in verses 23–29 is especially strong. God pierces them with His arrows (vv. 24–25) and consigns them to utter darkness (v. 26). But these metaphors are not accidental. They are directed at Job, who had already described himself as heading into a land of darkness (10:21–22) and God as coming upon him like a warrior (16:14). As if to give Job one final slap in the face, he says of the wicked, "The possessions of their house will be carried away, dragged off in the day of God's wrath" (NRSV). This too, of course, recalls what had happened to Job's possessions.

- ■ *Zophar makes an eloquent speech on the fate*
- ■ *of the wicked, but once again it misses the*
- ■ *mark because his thinly veiled attacks on*
- ■ *Job's character are wrong.*

JOB OPENS THE THIRD CYCLE (21:1–34)

This chapter represents the apex of Job's challenge to the conventional wisdom of the three friends. Here he moves beyond his own case, that of a righteous man suffering unjustly, and describes what he sees in the world: The wicked sin with impunity and receive no punishment. His language is surprising, even shocking, to find in the Bible. But he is grabbing his friends by the back of the neck and forcing them to look at situations they have studiously ignored. In outline, the speech is in two parts:

1. Job asks to be given a hearing (21:2–6)
2. The triumph of the wicked (21:7–34)

Compared to some of Job's other opening remarks, this one (vv. 2–6) is rather gentle. He does not rail against the friends or insult them; he simply asks them to bear with him a little while longer before mocking him anymore. This gentleness, however, is subtle. Job is about to rock their core values to the foundations, and he is inducing them to lower their guard with his opening remarks. It is noteworthy that in this speech Job departs from his usual pattern. He does not describe his own suffering and he does not pray. Here, he focuses entirely on bringing down their arguments. He is not being unfair to them, however, for he gives them advance notice that they will find his words upsetting. He declares that he has a case against God (v. 4). More importantly, he urges them to look at him and be appalled (v. 5). Job means more than that they should be stunned at how sick he is or how far he is fallen. *Job in his person represents the collapse of their theological system.* He is living proof that the theology of retribution has real problems and that they had better rethink how they live and what they believe. In fact, Job himself finds that the implications of recent events in his life have profoundly shaken him (v. 6).

Job begins his account with a portrait of the joys of the wicked (vv. 7–16). They live long, have healthy children, maintain their property, see increases in their net worth, enjoy life, and ignore God. This portrait is similar to Eliphaz's portrait of the joys of the righteous in 5:17–27. Throughout this speech, in fact, Job alludes to,

It is always frightening to come up against brute facts that seem to shake our beliefs to the core. It is never appropriate, however, to respond to these challenges with lies and anger. That is how Job's three friends met the uncomfortable facts that Job presented them. If we respond honestly in faith, God will lead us to deeper faith and greater truths.

parodies, or rebuts the speeches of the friends. He explicitly denies, for example, Bildad's assertion that the wicked die childless (v. 8; see 18:19). Verse 16 is somewhat surprising in this context since it seems to affirm a more traditional theology. We probably should understand it to mean that Job is not affirming that the way of the wicked is right, merely that it is often successful.

Bildad had claimed that the lamp of the wicked is put out (18:6). Job challenges both this and the traditional teaching that evil people are driven away like straw in the wind (vv. 17–18; see also Ps. 1:4). For Job, examples of godless people who prosper are so common over against the cases of them being swept away that it is hard to say which is the rule and which is the exception. Job has nothing but contempt for the retort that God punishes the children of the wicked. Such a course of action is meaningless to people since they do not care what will happen after they are gone. One could even say that such deferral of punishment to future generations even encourages evil behavior (vv. 19–21).

Job strengthens his case by pointing out that death is the great leveler of all people (vv. 23–26). He describes two men. The first is prosperous, financially secure, virile, and healthy. The second has had a life of failure and bitterness and has never enjoyed the good things that are common to people. His was a wretched life. Both men die, however, and both are eaten by worms. Whatever distinction existed between them is erased. Notably, Job does not assert that either man was good or bad, wise or unwise. They were simply fortunate and unfortunate. Job's point is that even if one could demonstrate that the righteous are more prosperous and healthy than the wicked, it would not matter. All end up in the grave together. Apart from a resurrection, it is hard to see where there could be any final justice.

Job anticipates and rebuts their answer to him in verses 27–34. They will, in typical fashion, claim that the houses of the mighty and the evil have disappeared ("Where is the house of the prince?" v. 28, NRSV). Job considers this naïve. The traveler, here representing the man of wide experience, can give them many examples of rich and crooked people who have held on to their power and pleasures well (vv. 29–30). The mighty live without fear of reproach and even approach death with a degree of satisfaction, knowing that they will have great tombs that are well cared for (vv. 31–33).

Thus, Job considers all the high-flown arguments of his friends worthless (v. 34). The facts simply do not support their doctrine. What are we to make of this? It is not that Job or the friends are wrong; it is that neither has comprehended what God's work of establishing justice really means. Job's case is better than that of the friends in that he is honest and they are not. But Job will not understand the truth until he hears the voice of God.

The Hebrew of 21:24 has an expression that is difficult but seems to mean, translating literally, "His intestines are full of milk." This could mean that he is well fed and fat, a condition that the ancients regarded as desirable (see Dan. 1:15). The translations attempt to interpret the line in various ways (The NIV, for example, says, "his body well-nourished.") On the other hand, it is possible that this is an example of how the Bible uses roundabout expressions to describe what modern, Western language would state more directly. If so, then the "intestines" refer to the male genitals, and "milk" refers to semen. The point is that these men are virile and sexually active. This, combined with the assertion that their "marrow" is "moist" describes a man who is physically healthy.

- In this text, Job determines once and for all to
- put the friends to silence. He bluntly
- describes the facts of life for them: The
- wicked do not all die young, childless, and
- poor. To the contrary, many live a full life
- without a thought of God and go to their
- graves with their sins unpunished. Whatever
- the truth is, Job will not understand the jus-
- tice of God by listening to his friends.

ELIPHAZ'S THIRD RESPONSE (22:1–30)

Eliphaz is a model for reactionary behavior. His zeal to defend traditional, orthodox teaching has brought him to the point of speaking words that are vicious, untrue, and at times contrary to sound theology. He began by mildly trying to win Job over to his position (chaps. 4–5), but when Job persisted in (truthfully) maintaining his innocence, Eliphaz's ire exceeded all bounds of decency. He could not deal with facts that seemed to upset his worldview.

The truth is ultimately never opposed to God and sound theology, but sometimes it seems to be. The true quality of a believer's character, whether humbly devout (because faith is strong) or fiercely reactionary (because faith is weak) comes to light on such occasions. Eliphaz's speech is divided as follows:

1. Job's sins (22:2–10)
2. God's justice (22:11–19)
3. A call for repentance (22:21–30)

Eliphaz begins with the most obviously unsound argument, that human acts of righteousness mean nothing to God (vv. 2–3). While it might be strictly true that human goodness does not really benefit God, the way Eliphaz puts it implies that God is simply indifferent to human conduct. The beginning of verse 2, "Can a man be of benefit to God?" seems to say that people are no more than vermin in God's eyes.

Beginning in verse 4, however, Eliphaz accuses Job of the most outrageous offenses against God and people, and the accusations are patently untrue. According to Eliphaz, Job has violated Deuteronomy 24:12–13 and kept the garments of the poor as security for loans (v. 6), has shown no compassion to the starving (v. 7), and has been indifferent to widows and orphans (v. 9). According to Eliphaz, Job considered himself to be one of the privileged lords of the earth (v. 8). These are outrageous lies, but as far as Eliphaz is concerned, they must be true because these are the only things that can account for Job's recent downfall (vv. 10–11). Combined with verses 2–3, these verses contain a double condemnation of Job: You are nothing in the eyes of God (vv. 2–3), but worse than that, you are a wicked sinner (vv. 4–11).

In addition, Eliphaz has a ready explanation for why Job turned so wicked: He had lost all fear of God (vv. 12–20)! He reasoned that Job had supposed that because God was so high in heaven and so far removed from human activity, it did not matter what Job did. God would not see, care, or respond. This accusation is leveled at a man who regularly made burnt offerings on behalf of his children on the mere chance that one of them had slipped up on a feast day and privately cursed God (1:5)! But as far as Eliphaz is concerned, Job has joined the throngs of the wicked who say, "What can the Almighty do to us?" (v. 17). Destruction awaits

"If your neighbor is poor and has only a cloak to give as security, do not keep the cloak overnight. Return the cloak to its owner by sunset so your neighbor can sleep in it and bless you. And the LORD your God will count it as a righteous act" (Deut. 24:12–13, NLT).

such sinners, but the righteous (such as Eliphaz) can look on and mock (vv. 18–20).

Eliphaz concludes with another call for repentance (vv. 21–30) that would be wonderfully eloquent were it not so absurd. He is like a man pleading with a lifelong teetotaler to give up strong drink. Along the way, he tacitly accuses Job of placing his faith in money rather than in God (vv. 24–25). The conclusion of the Eliphaz speech contains yet another irony, however; he claims that, should he repent, Job's integrity will even mean salvation for the guilty (v. 30). This turns out to be true, and Eliphaz is one of the guilty whom Job will save!

Gold of Ophir

The mines at Ophir were renowned for their gold (1 Kings 10:11; 1 Chron. 29:4; Isa. 13:12; Ps. 45:9). Ophir may have been in southeastern Arabia or in Somaliland on the east coast of Africa.

■ *Eliphaz closes with a flurry of charges that*
■ *are as false as they are ridiculous, and he*
■ *unknowingly sets the stage for his own*
■ *humiliation before God and Job.*

JOB LOOKS FOR JUSTICE (23:1–24:25)

The tone of the opening of this speech offers a striking contrast to that of Eliphaz's last speech. Eliphaz had been defending God's justice, but his opening remarks made God sound like a removed, indifferent, and capricious deity. Job is complaining about what he believes to be a great injustice done against him, but his tone is still reverent and trusting. God is good, and he will not condemn the guiltless. At the same time, Job courageously faces the fact that Eliphaz avoids: Something is really wrong with the world. The structure of this speech is:

1. Job's frustration over not being able to confront God (23:2–17)
2. The hard facts of life (24:1–25)

At the beginning of his speech, Job once again laments the fact that he cannot confront God face-to-face and challenge Him regarding the justice of what has befallen him. He does, however, speak of God in a positive manner. He is dismayed and bewildered at what has happened to him, and he is sure that his case is right. Nevertheless, Job still believes in the fundamental justice of God; he is sure that God would give him a fair hearing and yield to the justice of his case if only he could find a way to get to God (vv. 2–7). Job himself is the "upright man" of verse 7 who would win if given a chance. At this point, Job himself has still not moved beyond the theory of retributive justice endorsed by the three friends, and he still differs from them only in that he knows that he does not deserve what has come to him. When he does get to confront God, the actual outcome will be quite different from what Job has imagined.

God is an invisible adversary who makes His presence known by buffeting Job but who eludes direct contact (vv. 8–9). Nevertheless Job maintains his innocence. In contrast to Eliphaz, who claimed that Job had placed his faith *in gold* (22:24–25), Job asserts that when tested, he will be found to be as pure *as gold* (23:10).

In this light we must read the dramatic declarations of chapter 24, in which Job proclaims bluntly that injustice occurs everywhere in the world on a regular basis. Like the little boy who shouted that the emperor had no clothes on, Job exposes the blatant but ignored absurdity that the three friends constantly trumpet: The wicked are always punished, and the righteous always prosper. Once and for all, Job declares that this simply is not so. But his words are not those of a bitter man who has abandoned all faith in divine justice or who is ready to follow his wife's advice to "curse God and die."

In words that echo Eliphaz's ridiculous charges, Job asserts that people who really do what Eliphaz described often go unpunished while Job, who is innocent, lies crushed in the dirt. The wicked steal land and livestock (24:2). They abuse widows and orphans (24:3; see 22:9). They take away the clothing of the poor and leave them exposed to the elements (24:4–9; see 22:6). They pay no attention to the thirst of their wretched employees (24:10–11; see 22:7). Truly, these people have no fear of God and no desire to stay in right paths. Their numbers include murderers, adulterers, thugs, and housebreakers (24:13–17; see 22:12–17). In short, the world is full of unrequited evil.

The last eight verses of this speech (24:18–25), confuse readers. It appears as though Job has switched sides and decided that the world really is a just place because the wicked are transitory and their wealth is fleeting. Compounding the problem is that the Hebrew is difficult here, and at points translations differ considerably. Some interpreters say that these words cannot be Job's at all and attribute them to Zophar or Bildad. Some say it is an interpolation by a pious editor.

Interpolation

A short text inserted into a book by a later editor who generally has the purpose of upholding traditional theology. An "interpolation" is a text the original author of the book (supposedly) did not write.

It is not necessary to resort to these tactics, however. Some suggest that everything from verse 18 to the end of the chapter should be translated as a series of curses rather than as declarative statements. One could argue that verse 19, for example, ought to be translated, "As the drought and heat snatch the moisture of snow, so let Sheol snatch away those who sin." In this case, Job is not really saying that the wicked *do* wilt and die; he is only saying that he *wishes* they would die.

Even if this suggestion is rejected, however, and one takes the words to mean that Job believes that the wicked really do shrivel and die (as in the NRSV, NIV, and KJV), this does not mean that Job suddenly believes that all is right with the world. Job knows that wickedness can destroy one's life and that evil people perish in their sin. The problem is that justice is not consistently delivered in an observable manner. The wicked may wilt away, but many others (especially the poor) wilt away, too. Powerful and cruel people may thrive for a while and then vanish, but this does not happen in a way that allows observers to draw moral lessons. Job here almost sounds like Ecclesiastes: All is vanity, and people live out a life of madness and desperation, and then they vanish away. This is not, Job implies, a world where justice obviously rules! It is simply a world of vanity and wickedness.

■ *Job is frustrated by his inability to have an*
■ *audience with God, where he is sure he could*
■ *win his case. He looks at the world and sees*
■ *evil flourishing everywhere. The wicked do*
■ *perish, but this does not happen in a way that*
■ *demonstrates a moral center to the universe.*

BILDAD'S THIRD RESPONSE (25:1–6)

The surprising thing about this speech is that it is so short. By the standards of the book of Job, Bildad has barely gotten warmed up when he suddenly falls silent. Furthermore, his speech lacks elements we often see in the friends' speeches, such as a direct attack on Job's integrity and a call for him to repent. For these reasons many consider the text here to be corrupt. That is, it seems that part of Bildad's speech was accidentally moved somewhere else in the book or simply lost altogether. One could speculate, for example, that 24:18–25 was originally Bildad's text but that it accidentally was moved over to Job's section.

Corrupt text

Sometimes ancient scribes made errors as they laboriously made copies of books of the Bible by hand. Sometimes it is fairly obvious that a letter or word has been copied incorrectly. When a modern scholar speaks of a "corrupt text," the meaning is that the text has more than a few copyist's errors.

Once again, it is by no means necessary to assume that the text has been transmitted incorrectly, and at any rate it does no good since any attempt to fix it would be purely speculative. Probably we should understand the brevity of Bildad's speech to mean that Job has cut him off. Job has no reason to think he will hear anything new or useful from Bildad or the other two, so there is no point in sitting through another tiresome discourse. The anger and sarcasm of Job's opening words in 26:2 are another sign that he had lost all patience and interrupted Bildad.

We are indeed in familiar territory with Bildad's third speech. His entire message is a repeat of what Eliphaz had already asserted in his first speech: God is so high and holy that nothing, not even the angels, is pure in His sight. How much more impure are humans, who are made from dirt, in God's eyes? See 4:17–19 for Eliphaz's version of this idea. The concept may be true, but it misses an important point. What if the purity of the angels is not their own but is a reflected glory and purity derived from God Himself? In that case, the glory of the angels that God beholds is in fact His own glory, and He would not regard them as unclean. How much more, then, might this be the case with mortals? If the righteousness of God can be imputed or imparted to humans, then it is not our impurity but His glory that God sees in us. Bildad's theology is accurate as far as it goes, but it has no place for the saving righteousness of God.

- *In this text, Bildad's argument is that because*
- *God reigns from on high, has throngs of*
- *heavenly angels at His command, and is the*
- *source of all light, then nothing could be*
- *bright, awesome, or pure in His sight, least of*
- *all humans.*

JOB'S LAST ADDRESS TO THE FRIENDS (26:1–27:23)

In a book full of strange and disorienting speeches, Job's last address to his friends may be the strangest of all. The reason is that so much of it sounds like something the three friends would say themselves. In 26:5–14, Job speaks of God's mysterious power over the heavenly bodies, a power that made Him infinitely more holy than any human and thus free to treat them as He will. In 27:8–23, Job describes the destruction of the wicked in terms that match the ferocity and zeal of the three friends at their most eloquent. So surprising is this that many interpreters again conclude that the text has been corrupted and that this material is not where it belongs. Put another way, some scholars claim that speeches that originally belonged to Bildad or Zophar have been attributed to Job through scribal error. This seems all the more likely when one notices that Zophar is missing entirely in the third cycle. Rather than explain why Job sounds so much like the friends, all one has to do is give the unusual parts of his speeches back to Bildad and Zophar.

Again, however, this strategy does not work. Our task is to *interpret* and not to *edit* the book of Job. Furthermore, there are strong indications that there is no corruption here but that Job really is the speaker of these speeches. First, the structure of Job's speeches follows this pattern:

1. Job's outburst against Bildad (26:2–4)
2. The mystery and grandeur of God (26:5–14)
3. Job's insistence of his innocence (27:2–7)
4. The fate of the wicked (27:8–23)

We notice that Job begins both chapter 26 and chapter 27 with a defiant rejection of the friends' advice (26:2–4; 27:2–7) and then in both cases follows his outburst with a speech that sounds much like what the friends would say (26:5–14; 27:8–23). The reason Bildad's last speech is so short and Zophar has no third speech at all is now clear: *Job is giving their speeches for them.* He knows their doctrine so well he can recite it in his sleep. Having told them bluntly what he thinks of all they have said to him, he mimics their speeches, but with some subtle twists. What better way could Job have found to bring this tiresome debate to an end and get his friends to give it up and be quiet? We should also observe that verses that certainly belong to Job naturally lead into the speeches that mimic the friends' speeches. For example, in 27:7, after Job has vowed not to abandon his claim to innocence, he declares, "May my enemies be like the wicked, my adversaries like the unjust." It is clear that Job's "enemies" are his three friends. We, therefore, can understand why he immediately moves into a speech on the disasters that befall the wicked: Job is turning the tables and giving a warning to his friends!

At the opening of his speech (26:2–4), Job launches into an attack on Bildad, who was the last to speak. It appears that these remarks are indeed pointed directly at Bildad, because "you" in Hebrew is singular, not plural. The tone is highly sarcastic, as befits one who is fed up and not willing to hear any more useless advice. In verse 4, Job wonders what "spirit" gave such "wisdom." We can imagine him at this point casting a sideways glance at Eliphaz, the one who claimed to have learned deep theology from a divine visitor (4:12–16).

In 26:5–6, Job takes up the theme of the spirit world and at the same time picks up where Bildad left off. Bildad had spoken of God in the heights of heaven (25:2); Job claims that God looks into the heart of Sheol.

Job contends that God controls all the unseen, terrifying powers of death, chaos, and the abyss. God founded sky and earth on the chaos of nothingness (26:7) and can cause the pillars of heaven to tremble (26:11). God also controls the dragon creatures of the deep (26:12–13). For Job, all of this is to say, "Yes, I know what you are going to say: God is mighty and He controls all the forces of hell." Here, however, an irony is in store for Job. He has focused on how God manages mysterious and chaotic powers, including the great dragon. But when God speaks, Job will discover just how significant it is that God rules these creatures. Inasmuch as these ideas come back ironically upon Job's head, it is clear that he—not Bildad—is the speaker.

One last time Job announces that he will not yield on the fact that he did not commit some sin to deserve what befell him (27:2–7). In fact,

Abaddon

Abaddon occurs six times in the Hebrew Bible. KJV and NIV translate *Abaddon* as "destruction," while NASB and RSV retain the word *Abaddon*. It appears in parallel with Sheol and death and represents the dark side of existence beyond death.

for Job it would have been a lie to confess that he had sinned (27:4)! The amazing thing is that when Job at last confronts God, he still does not have to confess to having committed some sin. He realizes, however, that this is not the real issue and abandons any thought of challenging God.

Job's speech on the fate of the wicked is fairly typical, as he in fact intended it to be (27:8–23). Job's speech here is surprising and sarcastic: The wicked lose their children and all their possessions when fury comes upon them like a whirlwind. This describes what has just happened to him. Why would Job depict the fate of the wicked in terms so cruelly reminiscent of his own story? He has just announced his refusal to yield on the matter of his innocence, so this cannot be an acknowledgment of guilt on his part. It is best to read this as a sarcastic rehearsal of how the friends have made thinly veiled attacks on Job's character.

■ *Job puts his companions to silence in an*
■ *angry, sarcastic speech. He effectively muz-*
■ *zles them by parroting their doctrine back in*
■ *their faces. What Job did not expect is that*
■ *God would use Job's teaching about how God*
■ *controls the dragon of the deep to bring Job*
■ *himself to his knees.*

A HYMN TO WISDOM (28:1–28)

Scholars debate over who ought to be regarded as the speaker of this poem. Sandwiched between Job's final discourse to his friends (26:1–27:23) and his concluding words (29:1–31:40), one could easily take chapter 28 to be a continuation of Job's speech. The tone, however, is altogether unlike the vexed and agonized recitations we have heard Job give. Although chapter 28 expresses some despair over human ability to attain wisdom, it is calm and reflective in tone. Furthermore, if it is Job's, it seems to have him prematurely reconciled to the "fear of Yahweh," before his encounter with God from the whirlwind. Finally, it lacks the characteristic, "And Job said," that appears at the head of his other major speeches. All in all, it does not appear that Job is the speaker.

If it is not Job's speech, then whose is it? It can hardly be Zophar's missing third speech; it is too contemplative to represent the thoughts of any of the three friends, least of all the volatile Zophar. The text has not yet introduced either Elihu or God as speakers, so they too are eliminated. This chapter must be regarded as a kind of interlude given by the narrator. The content of the poem and its position in the book bear out this conclusion. The four sages have exhausted one another in the quest to resolve the dilemma posed by Job's affliction, and none has won the day. In short, their wisdom has failed them. Henceforth, the three friends have nothing more to say, and Job has nothing to say to them. Job's concluding speech (29:1–31:40) is not a parting shot—a final attempt to get his viewpoint across—it is a lament by a man who has lost everything and feels he no longer understands anything. The wisdom poem of chapter 28, as an interlude between the bitter debate with the friends and the final speeches of the book, invites us to consider whether the fear of God is a deeper wisdom than all the knowledge of the learned. When human

"The fear of the LORD is the beginning of knowledge" (Prov. 1:7, NASB).

understanding has failed us, we must await a word from God.

The poem is divided as follows:

1. The human activity of mining (28:1–11)
2. Wisdom is inaccessible (28:12–22)
3. God and wisdom (28:23–28)

Chapter 28 surprises us at the outset by devoting so much attention to the work of mining for minerals and precious stones (vv. 1–11). The poem lists a number of the things miners seek: gold, silver, iron, copper, and sapphires. It describes the lengths to which people will go to attain these precious materials: They leave the company of other humans and go into the depths of the earth, into the blackest darkness, where they expend immense effort, even to the point of overturning mountains, to find the riches of the earth. They go into places no wild animal knows or desires to visit. This is, of course, highly ironic. People will spare no effort, and they even go into the most horrible and unnatural places in order to attain wealth. They will not do the same for wisdom. But there is another, deeper irony as the text constructs a "pseudo-sorites": Even if they did dig for wisdom with the same energy they put into seeking gold, they would not find it.

Wisdom does not reside in the domain of humans. It is found neither among the living (v. 13) nor in Abaddon (v. 22). One cannot find it in any place, even in the depth of the sea (v. 14) or in the air, among the birds (v. 21). No amount of gold or jewels can purchase it. Once again, the text goes out of its way to give details; in the list of things that cannot buy wisdom, the following are included: gold, silver, onyx, sapphire, jewels, coral, pearls, and chrysolite.

Pseudo-sorites

This is a rhetorical device one sometimes sees in the Old Testament. It basically says, "X is not true, but even if it were, it would not matter." In this text, the implied pseudo-sorites is: "People do not seek for wisdom with the kind of intensity with which they seek gold, but even if they did seek wisdom, they would not find it."

These materials are, of course, the outcome of the work of mining, a task already portrayed as strenuous, dangerous, and unnaturally demanding. The point behind all this detail is that the finest metals and gems are useless for attaining wisdom; by implication, the most strenuous effort a person can put forth to gain it is equally futile. The text all but leaves one with a sense of despair at this point; humans appear to be a race of fools who work indefatigably for that which has little value but who do not have the slightest hope of gaining what really matters.

But all does not end in despondency; God does know the way to wisdom (v. 23). He understands everything about the physical world (that is, He is omniscient, vv. 24–27). He has declared to us, however, wherein true wisdom consists: Authentic wisdom is the fear of the LORD and the rejection of evil (v. 28). The proverb that the fear of the LORD is the beginning of wisdom is the keystone of the biblical theology of wisdom (e.g., Prov. 1:7). At this point in Job, however, this concept carries special importance. The fear of the LORD is the heart of true wisdom *even for those who are learned and orthodox in theology.*

In saying that wisdom does not reside among Abaddon, the powers of death, the text implies that one should not seek truth from the dead, as is done in séances.

Sometimes orthodoxy carries with it a hidden peril, like a dangerous side effect in a medicine that otherwise is good. The peril is in thinking that one understands the truth and even God better than one really does (or at least better than the wicked and unbelieving understand it). As such, the orthodox are prone to anger and absurd obstinacy when confronted with a situation they cannot readily explain.

■ *Chapter 28 is an interlude in the form of a*
■ *poem about wisdom. It teaches that humans*
■ *will expend enormous effort to attain riches*
■ *but will not do the same to attain wisdom, but*
■ *even if they did seek it, true wisdom is beyond*
■ *them. The deepest wisdom is the fear of God,*
■ *wherein one trusts Him rather than one's*
■ *own ability to comprehend life.*

JOB'S FINAL DISCOURSE (29:1–31:40)

Job concludes his speeches with a three-part discourse, as follows:

1. Job's former glory (29:2–25)
2. Job's present humiliation (30:1–31)
3. Job's negative confession (31:1–40)

Job begins his final speech with a pathetic yearning for his former glory (29:2–25). Occupying a full chapter of the book, we cannot but wonder what function this lamentation has in the structure of the whole. Is this simply a time of self-pity, meant to show that Job has become absorbed in his sorrows? If so, it would imply that Job has become so selfish that the larger issues of the justice of God and human suffering no longer matter to him. He just wants all the fame and wealth that he had before. In short, this interpretation implies that at this point, Job just wants to have the good life again and does not care about the deeper theological issues involved.

Negative Confession

A statement whereby an individual proclaims himself innocent of a series of offenses. It is called a "negative confession" because the individual gives a list of sins he has not committed instead of sins he has committed.

Such an interpretation, however, is too harsh. Throughout the dialogues, Job's fundamental concern has been that his theology and worldview have collapsed. As far as Job could tell, God had shown Himself to be capricious and had not behaved with justice. Furthermore, the "negative confession" of chapter 31, the words with which Job concludes, show that justice, not his own comforts, remain at the center of his concern. Thus, we should not dismiss chapter 29 as self-pity but should seek for its larger function in the book. That function seems to be to show that Job no longer has any theological missiles to hurl or arguments to build. He is at the end of his rope. He understands nothing of what has happened to him, and he can now only mourn.

Job is left with only three facts, and he enunciates each of these in turn: His life was once wonderful (chap. 29); it is now horrible beyond belief (chap. 30); and he has done nothing to deserve this (chap. 31). He gives powerful expression to his sorrow over how much he has lost, but at the heart of his grief is the fact that God has turned against him, and he does not know why.

What constituted the glory of Job's former days is the fact that those were the days when God was with him (29:2–6). When God cared for him, all was right in his world. Now, unaccountably, God has destroyed his world. The second half of verse 4 could be translated, "when the confidential friendship of God was upon my household." Now, God is his enemy. It is this fact, not the mere loss of possessions, that has Job completely bewildered. In verse 6, he declares that in those days his steps were drenched in milk and the rock poured out oil for him.

Like the familiar description of the land of Israel as "flowing with milk and honey," milk and oil here represent not just great abundance but especially God's favor.

In remembering his former glory, Job gives far more attention to the respect he had from one and all as a wise counselor than he gives to remembering his lost wealth. The public square in 29:7 is the place of deliberation. There, all gave deference to Job. Both the brash young men and the experienced old men gave him special honor, and counselors shut their mouths when he spoke. In other words, everyone held Job's words in the highest esteem. His advice was valued (29:7–10, 21–25). Here again, it is precisely as wise sage that Job has been undone. Far from being able to respond wisely, Job finds himself confronting a crisis for which he has no answers at all.

Defending the weak

The Old Testament and ancient wisdom generally heavily stress the need for people of power and wealth to defend the weak, needy, and oppressed. King Lemuel's mother urged him to speak up for and protect the destitute (Prov. 31:8–9), and the prophets regularly demanded that people care for the widows and orphans. In claiming to have done this, Job claims to have met the primary duty that is laid upon the upper classes.

People especially revered Job for his compassion. The poor, the orphan, the widow, the dying, the infirm, and victims of crime and injustice all looked to him for help (29:11–17). These persons represent every category of needy person toward whom the righteous was supposed to show compassion. And Job did not fail to do his duty. All found him to be a good man toward whom they could turn when in need.

Because he lived in this manner, Job assumed that God would do His part and protect him. He thought that he would die in his own home (29:18, literally "nest"), meaning that he would not lose his home due to poverty and perhaps that he would be surrounded by family in his death. Job had lived like the wise man of Psalm 1, who is totally devoted to God and who flourishes like a tree planted by a river. Thus, Job expected to have his roots spread out to the water (29:19). But his hope was not vindicated; his root had dried up; and it seemed that the promise had failed.

Chapter 30, Job's lament over his current condition, is in three parts. First, he proclaims that the dregs of society now delight in mocking his fall from honor (30:1–15). In fact, it is not even the dregs of society but, lower still, their children who taunt him in their songs! This contrasts with how he was previously revered by even the noblest in the land. In 30:2–8, Job describes these people who now make fun of him. They are outcast, homeless, unfit for any job, and living like animals among the scrub of the desert. Decent people chase them away as they would thieves or a pack of wild dogs (30:5). Verse 8 literally calls them "sons of stupidity, sons of the nameless." In other words, they are nobodies, and deservedly so. Yet even these people have abandoned all pretense of respect for Job. They spit at his presence (v. 10). This insult represents more than personal hostility; it implies that they regard him as one whom God has cursed. Job shares their opinion (30:11). How much more, the text implies, have the middle and upper classes come to regard him with disdain.

The second part of Job's lament concerns the more fundamental reversal, that God Himself is against Job (30:16–23). While his afflictions tear him to pieces and bring him down into dust (vv. 16–19), God not only stands aloof from Job's prayers for help but positively adds to his suffering (vv. 20–23). Although the Hebrew of verse 22 is somewhat obscure, it seems that God comes upon Job like a storm and tosses him to and fro. This ironically reverses the image of God coming with the whirlwind to save His people and destroy His enemies (e.g., Ps. 77:18). Here, for reasons he does not understand, Job has become God's enemy. This idea contains another irony unknown to Job, however: In 38:1, God will speak to Job out of the whirlwind, but it will ultimately be for his salvation rather than his destruction.

In the third part of his complaint in chapter 30, Job contends that God has not treated him with the same level of compassion that Job has shown to others (vv. 24–31). As a matter of principle, one should be compassionate to those who have suffered disaster (v. 24), and Job himself did not fail in this regard (v. 25). But he did not receive the same when evil befell him (v. 26). By implication, it is God who should have given Job this kind of mercy. Instead, he has become like the outcasts described in verses 1–15. A creature of the desert, he dwells among wild beasts without shelter and scorched by the sun.

In chapter 31, Job abruptly turns to the negative confession with which he ends his words. Here, he solemnly declares that he is innocent of all offenses that might have merited the punishment he received. It is critical to recognize that everything Job says here is valid. More than that,

God and the Storm

The Old Testament often describes God as coming upon His enemies in the fury of a storm or whirlwind. At times He comes to save Israel (Ps. 77:18; Zech. 9:14), but Israel can also receive the fury of the storm if it is in sin (Jer. 4:13). Here Job feels that he is treated as one of God's hated enemies.

Negative Confession

An example of a negative confession would be Job's saying, "If I have stolen my neighbor's land, then may my own land grow only thorns." There is a sense in which he is swearing to his own harm if he has done certain things. In this form, the *if* clause is called the protasis. The *then* clause is the apodosis.

Old Testament believers knew that lust was destructive to one's soul and spiritual life. To induldge in lust is to risk losing all the good things God has for us.

as we shall see, it does no good to weigh in with pious judgments that although Job was indeed a good man, he still had some lessons to learn. Again, chapter 1 plainly states that Job's sufferings came upon him because of his righteousness, not because he had some areas, however small, that needed improvement.

Speaking in the form of the negative confession, Job solemnly avows that he has not committed the sin described. In this chapter, he cites fourteen types of sin he has not fallen into, a number that is significantly twice seven, a number that is important in apocalyptic thought and signifies completion. The implication of the whole is that his moral character has been wholly flawless, a point that the prologue has already established.

The first sin he had avoided is lust (vv. 1–2). The "covenant with the eyes" he describes is a commitment he had made to turn his eyes away from looking upon a young woman lustfully. Verse 2 implies that to engage in lust is to forfeit one's "heritage" from God, a word that is suitably ambiguous. It can mean everything from divine favor in this life to eternal rewards. Possibly, the "heritage" he would lose by indulging in lustful leering at young women would be marital happiness and sexual contentment.

The second sin about which Job claims innocence is general in nature: He disavows being a "worker of iniquity" (vv. 3–4). In Proverbs, many texts simply teach that a person should not do evil, so such a generic statement is not surprising or out of place here. Once again, the fear of God dominates this text: God sees every step he takes, and therefore, he must be careful how he lives. This passage tells us that the "fear of God" includes real fear of divine displeasure.

The third sin Job disavows is living a life of lies (vv. 5–6). The idea of hastening toward deceit reminds one of the seven deadly sins of Proverbs 6:16–19, a list that includes a lying tongue and feet that hasten to do evil. The curse Job calls down on himself, that he should be weighed in a "just balance," implies that the kind of deceit he especially has in mind is cheating others in business. In ancient Israel, business fraud often involved using unbalanced scales and improper weights in transactions (see Prov. 20:23).

The fourth sin is simply turning aside from the way, or apostasy (vv. 7–8). This too is fairly general in nature; it could refer to abandoning the faith, but the emphasis is on turning aside from perseverance in doing good. The penalty described in the apodosis is appropriate. Just as the apostate abandons his loyalty to God and to doing what is right, so also the apostate should lose the benefits of being under God's care. In the Old Testament, the produce of the land is the sign of God's faithfulness to His people.

The fifth sin is adultery (vv. 9–12). In the apodosis (v. 10), Job declared that if he has committed such an act, another man should "bow over my wife" (that is, have sexual intercourse with her). He then goes on to declare why this is such a terrible offense. First, it is an act worthy of criminal judgment. That is, he has violated both his marriage vow and that of another man and wife. Second, he says that it is a fire that burns all one's harvest.

The sixth sin is cruelty toward or indifference to the needs of one's slaves (vv. 13–15). The apodosis asserts that both he and his slaves are creatures of God and thus that he has no right to

Fear of God

Today, people are quick to assert that the "fear of God" means "reverence for God." While this is true, the concept should not be diluted with notions of an indulgent God. There is an element of real "fear" in the fear of God because God sees and punishes sin.

Let me sow and another eat

In the prophets, God frequently warns the nation that if they persist in being faithless to the covenant, He will take away their heritage, the land and its produce. See, for example, Hosea 2:8–9. Job, similarly, says another should take the produce of his land if he is apostate.

The idea seems to be that sexual indiscretion is a passion that destroys those who let it get out of control and can even bring them to financial ruin. See Proverbs 6:25–35.

Hyperbole

A rhetorical device often used in the Old Testament in which the speaker exaggerates for effect. Hyperbole is not meant to be and should not be taken literally.

abuse a person who is made in God's image. It is noteworthy that Job considers both male and female slaves to have the right to have their complaints fairly heard and redressed.

The seventh sin is apathy about the suffering of the poor (vv. 16–23). As is common in texts of this kind, Job gives special attention to widows and orphans. In a world without social services, legal defense, or even a police force, widows and orphans were the most vulnerable members of society. The expression "from my mother's womb" simply means "all my life." It is an example of hyperbole and should not be taken literally; Job did not literally care for widows from the day he was born. In claiming that he has been a "father" to the orphans, Job means that he has cared for them and protected their interests. The apodosis, that his arm should be wrenched from its socket should he fail to do his duty here (v. 22), implies that just as the widow and the orphan are helpless, so too he should be rendered helpless should he not care for them.

The eighth sin is trust in wealth rather than in God (vv. 24–25). This text has no separate apodosis but shares a common apodosis with the ninth sin—idolatry—a sin to which greed is closely related (see Col. 3:5).

The ninth sin is idolatry and pagan religion (vv. 26–28). Looking at the sun and moon here is not mere admiration of nature but devotion to the heavenly bodies as gods. It is worshiping the creature rather than the Creator (Rom. 1:25). Similarly, the mouth kissing the hand represents some kind of pagan act of devotion, probably throwing a kiss to an idol. For both greed and idolatry, Job has a common verdict: they are faithlessness to God (v. 28).

The tenth sin is a spirit of spite and hatred, whereby one wishes the worst for one's enemies (vv. 29–30). So careful has Job been that he would not utter a curse against any person.

The eleventh sin is indifference to the stranger and sojourner (vv. 31–32). The translation of verse 31 is uncertain, but it seems to mean that no one who visited Job's tent had cause to say that he went away hungry. Verse 32 is more clear: No stranger had to spend the night in the street near Job's house. The importance of hospitality in the ancient Near East is illustrated by the account of Lot and the angels (Gen. 19:1–3).

The twelfth sin is hypocrisy (vv. 33–34), here described as keeping one's sin concealed out of fear of public opinion. This is a false piety that arises from desire to be accepted by people rather than a desire to please God.

A phony spirituality is even more abhorrent to God than it is to people. No one who has lived a life of false spirituality can claim to be innocent before God.

The thirteenth sin is not specified but, like the second, is a general assertion of Job's innocence (vv. 35–37). Job asks that God give him a detailed account of his sins if such sins exist. He would proudly display that list, not because he is proud of sin, but because such an indictment would allow him to make sense of all the calamity that has befallen him. His torment is in not knowing why all this has happened. At the same time, a clear accusation from God would allow him to proceed boldly before God ("like a prince") and make his defense.

The fourteenth sin seems anticlimactic after the bold demand of verses 35–37, that God openly accuse him of *something*. But the last sin is taking land or its produce by oppression and extortion (vv. 38–40), much as Jezebel took away Naboth's vineyard (1 Kings 21:7–15). To extort crops or land from tenant farmers or impoverished peasants was a heinous crime in the ancient world (see James 5:1–4). Job may have given this sin special place to put to silence speculation that he, a wealthy landowner, had enriched himself by this means.

■ *Job concludes his speeches with lamentation*
■ *and solemn declaration. He is a man who has*
■ *lived in perfect integrity, whom God once*
■ *protected, and who had every reason to*
■ *believe that God would continue to protect*
■ *him. But God has suddenly become his*
■ *enemy for no apparent reason. Job can only*
■ *lament his current condition and declare*
■ *that, as far as he can tell, his case calls into*
■ *question the whole idea of the justice of God.*

THE ELIHU SPEECH (32:1–37:24)

Out from nowhere a new speaker emerges, the young man Elihu. He makes the longest, uninterrupted series of speeches in the book, but no one responds to him or speaks about him. He vanishes as abruptly as he appears. Some scholars find it difficult to believe that the author would suddenly introduce a new speaker, have him claim that he has been present all along, allow him to give an enormously long and verbose discourse, and then drop him from the book without any comment at all. Nevertheless, the Elihu speeches play a significant but surprising role in the book; and they should be regarded as original. The structure of the Elihu speeches is as follows:

1. Elihu demands a hearing (32:6–33:7)
2. First response to Job: Some suffering is redemptive (33:8–33)

3. Second response to Job: Theology of retribution (34:1–37)
4. Third response to Job: God is above human sin and suffering (35:1–16)
5. Fourth response to Job: Theology of retribution (36:1–21)
6. Anticipation of an appearance of God (36:22–37:24)

According to 32:1–5, Elihu was the son of an otherwise unknown Barachel, of the tribe of Buz and clan of Ram. These names imply that he was of the desert country east of Israel.

Interpreters differ over whether Elihu should be regarded as a profound thinker who anticipates God and substantially solves the dilemma of Job or as a pompous buffoon who contributes virtually nothing original. Actually, both assessments of Elihu are a bit exaggerated; he is more the sophomore than the sage.

Those who seek to exonerate Elihu essentially have two arguments. First, they say that he has introduced a new idea, that suffering need not be punitive but can be disciplinary and redemptive. In this, he is supposed to have moved beyond the theology of retribution and to have reminded the others that sorrow can build character and increase piety. Second, they say that elements of Elihu's speech foreshadow God's speech, especially in chapter 37, where Elihu proclaims that God is coming in the whirlwind and asks Job if he can explain the mysterious workings of God (37:14–18).

These arguments, however, fail to demonstrate original wisdom in Elihu. First, the concept that the righteous must undergo disciplinary or redemptive suffering is not original to Elihu. Eliphaz had already made substantially the same point in his first speech at 5:17–19. It is rather strange, furthermore, to argue that God killed Job's children, took away all his possessions, and ruined his health in order to improve his character. Second, although Elihu begins by speaking of redemptive suffering (33:12–30), he soon falls into condemning Job as an unrepentant sinner in much the same way the three friends did (e.g., 34:7–9, 37; 36:5–21). Indeed, much of Elihu's speech is a rehash of what the three friends have already said, such as that God is not really affected by human righteousness or sin (35:6–8; see 22:2–3). Third, Elihu's theology, like that of the three friends, is orthodox but entirely off the mark in the case of Job. We already know that Job's afflictions did not come upon him in order to improve his character but precisely because he was righteous before God and Satan alike. However valid the theology of redemptive suffering may be, we know from the prologue that it is not the reason for Job's affliction. Like the three friends, Elihu refuses to believe that Job has done nothing wrong to merit the grief he has received, since that would upset the moral order of the universe (34:5–15). Elihu counsels Job to repent (36:11–17), but he does not reckon with the fact that in order to repent Job would have to fabricate some sin.

According to Proverbs 17:27–28, a wise man uses words with restraint, and even a fool is thought wise if he can keep his mouth shut. In fact, however, fools are notorious for being verbose and highly opinionated.

The second argument, that Elihu to some degree anticipates God's speech, is valid but not decisive. Elihu, like the reader, is looking for God to step in and clarify everything. God does appear, and He does bring Job to complete repentance, but it is repentance of a different sort than Elihu anticipates. As we shall see, God moves the discussion in an entirely new direction and in so doing removes all of Job's objections. Elihu's speech is a transition to God's, but it falls far short of the decisive conclusion that God brings about.

There is no escaping the fact that Elihu is unbelievably verbose and self-assured. He takes more than a full chapter just to introduce himself

(32:6–33:7), in the course of which he repeatedly makes the point that he is about to say something profound. He claims to have new insights (32:14), but he substantially repeats much that has already been said. He claims to be above allowing his words to be influenced by concern for the opinions of others (32:21–22), and he takes on the role of God's spokesman (33:6) and professes that he has "pure" knowledge (33:3). More than all that, he claims to be perfect in understanding (36:4)!

Elihu serves as a warning to the reader of this book. Like the reader, he is frustrated that no one can answer Job, and he is sure that it is not correct to challenge whether God righteously governs the world. At the same time, he knows that the three friends have failed in their attempt to convict Job of any specific sin. In addition, readers sometimes come to Job with a certain arrogance; they assume that they are qualified to assess the arguments and pass judgment concerning who was right and who was wrong. Like such readers, Elihu feels sure that he understands the situation better than do any of the four sages. But as he thrashes about for an answer, he makes many valid statements, yet he cannot bring the debate to a decisive conclusion. He rightly anticipates that God will resolve the situation, but he cannot foresee the direction God will actually go. In his attempt to answer Job, Elihu sounds suspiciously like the three friends, primarily because he has chosen to ignore the fact that Job really is righteous. This is how Elihu stands as a warning to the reader: *Those who fail to face squarely the dilemma of Job's case and who retreat into the idea that Job still had to have his character improved will inevitably come out on the side of the three friends.*

Often the actual value of a person's insights is *inversely* proportional to how highly that person esteems his or her insights. It is noteworthy that everybody ignores Elihu entirely; this does not speak very highly of the kind of impression he made.

After his appeal for a hearing (32:6–33:7), Elihu launches into his first argument, that God sometimes brings calamity on an individual to keep him from falling into sin (33:8–33). This argument is not really new in the book of Job, and it is not appropriate to Job's situation. In 33:8–11, Elihu summarizes Job's position that he has been severely punished although he has done no wrong. Elihu responds that God sends messages in the form of dreams and personal calamities to prevent people from turning to the wrong (33:12–22). Like Job, Elihu envisages a heavenly mediator who might intercede for an individual during his time of suffering (33:23–28), but he does not arise to the messianic vision Job had developed. Rather, Elihu's mediator is a special class of angel who has the assignment to carry out this function. Since the phrase "one of a thousand" (33:23) signifies something rare, it does not appear that he believes there are many such angels or that he places much hope in this kind of deliverance.

In his second answer to Job, Elihu again appeals for a hearing (34:1–4) and again summarizes Job's argument (34:5–9), but this time he adds a severe censure to Job in the process by asserting that he has joined the company of the wicked (v. 8). What follows is a traditional statement of the doctrine of retribution such as any of the three friends or Job himself could easily have made (34:10–30). Verse 11 fairly summarizes everything Elihu says here: "He [God] repays a man for what he has done; he brings upon him what his conduct deserves." It is difficult to avoid the conclusion, moreover, that Elihu is making veiled accusations against Job himself when he declares that God is aware of every hidden sin and suddenly shatters the mighty (vv. 21–25). In 34:31–37, he declares that the only cure is to repent, and he denounces Job for failure to do so.

After another summary of Job's position (35:1–4), Elihu declares that God can be sublimely indifferent to human behavior (35:5–16). It does not affect God one way or the other, he contends, whether Job does right or does wrong (vv. 5–8). Furthermore, God need not respond to the cries of the oppressed if the oppressed themselves are not among the righteous. How much less, then, could Job expect God to respond while Job remains in a state of impious anger (vv. 9–16)? The danger, of course, is that Elihu has taken two facts—the *aseity* of God and the fact that God demands that all submit to him—and has exaggerated these into a portrait of a God who almost ignores issues of justice and who has little regard for human suffering. Elihu's idea of God has almost moved beyond the idea of a sovereign deity; He is practically a god of caprice.

In his fourth response to Job, Elihu falls back on the theology of retribution (36:1–21) and seems to turn away from the almost indifferent God of the third response. Once again he appeals for his audience to pay attention, this time claiming in the most extravagant way that he possesses true wisdom (36:2–4). He then declares that God protects the pious but destroys the wicked (36:5–15). Once again, his words contain veiled accusations against Job. He contends that God maintains the righteous as "kings" but that should they fall into "fetters," God would tell them what transgressions they committed that merited this punishment (36:7–10). One need not be too imaginative to see that the man who lived as a king but fell into a prison of darkness

Elihu's third answer to Job is strange and perhaps serves as a warning that those who twist facts to preserve orthodoxy risk falling into an error greater than the one they are fighting.

Aseity

This is the orthodox doctrine that God cannot be changed by His creation. It prevents Christians from falling into a semipagan notion of a limited, changing god, but it can lead to distortions if exaggerated. Especially dangerous is the idea that God is indifferent to human actions.

was Job himself. Following Elihu's logic, it only remains for Job to recognize his sin and await instruction from God. Like the three friends, moreover, Elihu becomes increasingly strident and intemperate in his choice of words. He declares that all the wicked will die among the male prostitutes of the shrines (36:14). Apparently Job's skin disease has suggested to him the sexually transmitted diseases these prostitutes may have had. Elihu, too, has become cruel in his attempt to bring Job into submission.

Shrine prostitutes

These prostitutes were attached to the shrines of the fertility gods of the ancient Near East. People who came to worship at these shrines engaged in sexual acts with the prostitutes in order to arouse their gods and thus cause their fields and flocks to be more fertile.

Elihu closes with a warning to Job that he is in danger of falling into complete reprobation (vv. 16–21). He even supposed that Job would trust in riches to save him (v. 19; see NIV and NASB), something Job has never hinted at but that Eliphaz wrongly accused him of (22:24–25). Believing that he alone understands the case, Elihu misconstrues the situation completely.

Elihu closes his speech by anticipating the appearance of God in a whirlwind (36:22–37:24). Everything he says from this point on is theologically valid, and much of it is taken up again in God's speech. Like the three friends, Elihu is essentially orthodox and pious. This orthodoxy does not guarantee, however, that Elihu's overall understanding of the situation is correct. He opens with a general statement that God's power is overwhelming (36:22–26). From this, he moves into a description of the weather—especially storms—as reflections of the power and grandeur of God (36:27–37:13). He declares that the way God dispenses rain, thunder, and lightning is analogous to His governance of the world (36:27–33). For Elihu, this is an awesome spectacle. The weather frightens the animals as surely as it controls the activity of humans

(37:7–8). In 36:13, Elihu points out that by the same clouds God can either punish people (as in floods) or show them His love (as in giving water to the crops). He then challenges Job to place his wisdom against God's and see how pathetic Job's is (37:14–20). Can Job explain where lightning comes from? Does he understand principles of radiation, whereby heat is transferred from the sun to the clothing on his skin? Can Job spread out the skies? The obvious answer to all these questions is no. God will take up this line of questioning with Job, but He will take it in a different direction. He will not accuse Job of being a sinner but will force him to confront the inadequacy of his understanding of God and of justice.

Elihu closes his long speech with a doxology; God is inscrutable but good and full of glory (37:21–24). Curiously, though, he ends with a line in verse 24 that might be taken in either of two ways. With the NIV, one could take it to mean that God has regard for the wise in heart (that is, for those who fear God). Almost every other translation, however, takes the line negatively to mean that God has no regard for the wise in heart (that is, for those who are wise in their own conceit). This is probably the better translation. In a book as full of irony as Job, this remark surely contains irony. After all, who has been wiser in his own eyes than the prolix and pretentious Elihu?

■ *Elihu, like the reader, has observed the dia-*
■ *logue. Although he knows that the friends*
■ *have failed to convict Job of any sin, he is*
■ *incensed that Job would claim that the fury*
■ *that has come upon him represents a miscar-*
■ *riage of justice. Like many readers, he is con-*
■ *vinced he understands the situation better*
■ *than the four principle characters. He sets*
■ *about trying to prove Job wrong with the idea*
■ *of redemptive suffering but in the end parrots*
■ *much of what has already been said by the*
■ *friends. He concludes by extolling the divine*
■ *power that is revealed in the storm and*
■ *serves as a transition to God's speeches. In*
■ *the end Elihu, like the reader, is ignored by*
■ *all the other characters of the book.*

QUESTIONS TO GUIDE YOUR STUDY

1. Why did Job's three friends quit answering him?
2. What caused Elihu to be angry with Job?
3. What impression do you have of Elihu from his speeches?

GOD'S FIRST SPEECH (38:1–40:5)

God's speeches are perhaps not what the reader expected. They have almost nothing to say about justice, sin, or punishment. They do not, in fact, seem to address the fundamental questions of Job at all. Nevertheless, Job himself finds them totally compelling, so we must assume that God's words somehow answer the challenge Job intended to lay at God's feet. The divine speeches describe God's governance of the natural world but focus on its wilder, more uncontrollable aspects of nature. In structure, the speeches are composed of two interrogations (38:1–40:2; 40:6–41:34), after each of which Job submits (40:3–5; 42:1–6). In both cases, God begins by demanding that Job stand before Him "like a man" (38:2–3; 40:6–7). In the first speech God declares sixteen areas over which He is sovereign but in the second, only two. Nevertheless, there is a progression whereby the final two parts of God's second speech climax and explain the whole. The structure of the first speech is as follows:

1. Creation of the universe (38:4–7)
2. The sea (38:8–11)
3. The rising sun (38:12–15)
4. Sheol (38:16–18)
5. Light and darkness (38:19–21)
6. Storms (38:32–30)
7. Seasons and the stars (38:31–33)
8. Clouds (38:34–38)
9. Lions (38:39–40)
10. Ravens (38:41)
11. Mountain goats (39:1–4)
12. Wild donkeys (39:5–8)
13. Wild oxen (39:9–12)
14. Ostriches (39:13–18)
15. Horses (39:19–25)
16. Birds of prey (39:26–30)

The first area over which God claims sovereignty is creation itself (38:4–7). He describes the work of creating the world as though it were a building under construction, needing to have its dimensions marked off, its foundation laid, and footings and cornerstones set in. It is curious that the text speaks of the "morning stars" singing for joy along with the "sons of God" (that is, angels; 38:7). Normally, the morning stars are the planets Mercury and Venus, but here they seem to be another term for angels.

Sons of God

This term is a common expression for angels; it appears in Genesis 6:2, 4; Job 1:6; 2:1; 38:7. Some theologians have contended that God made the angels during the week of the creation of heaven and earth, but this text implies that they were created prior to the physical universe.

The Israelites were not a seafaring people and tended to regard it with dread. As a chaotic and threatening force, the sea anticipates the wild and dangerous creatures God must control, not the least of whom is the sea-dragon Leviathan.

Underworld

Several passages connect the physical underworld to Sheol, the world of the dead (Deut. 32:22; Job 17:16; Ps. 139:8; Amos 9:2). Readers need to be careful about taking literally what the Bible presents as poetic metaphor. We are not to understand the Bible to teach that Sheol literally exists inside the earth.

Obviously Job was not around at the beginning of creation, and he could not answer God's questions.

The second area of divine dominion is the sea (38:8–11). This text seems to be a poetic version of Genesis 1:9. Here God uses two altogether different metaphors. First, the sea came forth like a newborn baby needing to be wrapped in a blanket. Second, the sea is like a monster or prisoner who must be confined behind locked doors.

The third area about which God challenges Job is the function of sunrise (38:12–15). Here God does refer to the wicked but does not address the issue of punishing the wicked in the manner the three friends and Elihu have. Instead, God makes the point that the rising sun sends evildoers scattering (because they love the darkness) in the same way dust is taken out of a rug when it is shaken. The implication (which shall be developed in detail) is that God knows how to deal with the wicked but that His methods are not necessarily those described by the sages. In verse 14, the text speaks of daylight giving shape to the earth after the night has wrapped it in formless darkness. This is an event of joy and beauty, but the wicked will experience none of it (v. 15).

The fourth area of God's exclusive dominion is the underworld (38:16–18), here described both as the physical world underground (vv. 16, 18) and as the domain of the dead (v. 17). The deep subterranean world and the realm of the dead are both beyond Job's sphere of knowledge. By implication, God has power over death and thus over all aspects of ultimate justice.

The fifth area that Job could not explain is the nature of light and darkness (38:19–21). Modern physics has made some progress here but has found the quantum world of photons and radiation to be mysterious indeed. Light and darkness are metaphorical for good and evil, so once again God is pointing out to Job that God understands ultimate issues of right and wrong in a way that Job could never hope to do.

The sixth area God exclusively controls is the weather (38:32–30), an area Elihu had already touched upon in his speech (36:24–37:20). Once again the text describes the storm as both an agent of wrath and the means by which God gives water to crops. The point is that to manage properly the rain, hail, snow, and lightning, it requires great wisdom. God must take care that the weather is destructive or beneficial in the appropriate places. For Job, the message is that God knows what He is doing in dispensing justice. Also, there is an element of sheer wonder in the natural world, such as the formation of ice from water (v. 30).

The seventh area God exclusively controls is the changing of the seasons as observed in the constellations (38:31–33). Although this passage names various constellations, which constellations are being referred to is unclear.

On the fourth day, God created the heavily bodies to separate days, seasons, and years (Gen. 1:14). In this text, the fact that God controls the heavenly bodies further demonstrates His ability to govern the world.

The eighth area of God's governance is the clouds (38:34–38). This is similar to 38:22–30, except that there the focus was on weather systems generally and here it is on clouds specifically. Like soldiers, the clouds report to God when called upon with the words, "Here we

From whose womb did the ice come out?

Modern readers are surprised to read of the rain having a father and the hoarfrost a mother (38:28–29). These expressions are echoes of the myths, in which deities and fairies were supposed to generate natural phenomena. In the Bible, they have ceased being descriptions of supposedly real gods and have been demoted to mere poetic imagery.

Translations such as "Pleiades," "Orion," and "Bear" are educated guesses. Although the Bible rejects astrology, ancient peoples (including the Israelites) firmly believed that the stars in some way governed life, at least in terms of marking off the seasons of the year.

are!" (v. 35). Job's complete inability to control or even understand these things contrasts with God's absolute authority.

The ninth domain in which Job has no authority is the prides of lions (38:39–40). Here, for the first time, the governance of wild animals is the focus, and this theme will dominate the rest of God's speech. Lions are no doubt placed first because they are renowned for their ferocity. Even these powerful creatures are wholly subject to the will of God and dependent on Him. The theme that God can manage creatures which to humans seem beyond all control will be developed through the rest of God's address.

The tenth area of God's domain is among the ravens, who are likewise dependent on divine favor (38:41). Jesus spoke of God's provision for the sparrows in order to emphasize how God cares for the little things (Matt. 10:29). Here, the text mentions ravens because they are large, crafty birds, and the focus is on how God manages things that are wild and powerful.

Using a series of descriptions of animals that are wild and dangerous, God repeatedly makes the point that He alone can control forces of danger and evil. This anticipates the great beast of evil, Leviathan, in chapter 41.

The eleventh area of divine control is over the gestation of mountain goats (39:1–4). The ability to survive and even bear young among the crags of the mountains is a miracle in itself. The implied point is that God is able to sustain life even in the midst of the most hostile settings, and thus God can manage all forces hostile to life.

The twelfth domain that God manages is that of the wild donkeys (39:5–8). These creatures are proverbial for being unmanageable (Gen. 16:12; Jer. 2:24). A creature of the desert, the wild donkey scoffs at the idea of human control (v. 7). Yet it is God who gave him this freedom and God who sustains him. The lesson is that things that are beyond human ability to manage are entirely under God's command.

Wild donkeys are proverbial for being unmanageable (Jer. 2:24). This is why Ishmael is described as a wild donkey (Gen. 16:12); he operated outside of normal civilized society.

The thirteenth thing that God manages is the wild ox (39:9–12). The translation "wild ox" is subject to some debate (the KJV has "unicorn"). The beast in question here may be the aurochs, a wild ox that stood some six feet tall at the shoulders (extinct since 1627). Again, the point is that this beast cannot be tamed by humans and serves as a metaphor for God's ability to manage chaotic powers.

The fourteenth thing God alone controls is the ostrich (39:13–18). God describes this creature as not only powerful and untamable but also exceptionally brutish. The bird was renowned in antiquity for its lack of sense and its silly behavior, and the text takes up these popular ideas. Stupid creatures are inherently difficult to manage, but here, too, God is up to the task.

The fifteenth thing God controls is the horse (39:19–25). This creature is different from those mentioned above in that it does submit to human authority. The emphasis here, however, is on the power and bravery of the war horse with the point being that Job did not give the horse its great strength and spirit. The mere fact that there are things in the natural world that people can to some degree understand or manage does not put people on an equal footing with God. The horse's willingness to do battle, moreover, anticipates the greatest warrior beast of all, Leviathan (41:1–34).

The sixteenth area of God's domain is over the raptors (birds of prey; 39:26–30). Two features of the raptor receiving special attention are his ability to soar and his thirst for blood. One last time this text asserts that only God can control things that are wild, powerful, and dangerous. God asks Job if he is up to setting himself alongside God (40:1–2); and Job, anticipating his response in 42:1–6, declares that he is unworthy to confront God.

GOD'S SECOND SPEECH (40:6–41:34)

The entire first speech serves as prelude to the second, which brings God's argument to a gripping climax. It is in three parts, as follows:

1. Introduction: A Challenge to Job (40:6–14)
2. Behemoth (40:15–24)
3. Leviathan (41:1–34)

After again calling on Job to brace himself like a man (40:7), God challenges Job with what in essence is a single question: Are you capable of bringing justice into the world? In 40:8–14, Job reckons with the fact that he does not begin to have the power to bring evil under control and establish righteousness. He cannot clothe himself in glory and unleash his wrath against the evil. More is at stake than the fact that Job cannot hurl bolts of lightning against sinners. Many people smugly say something like, "If I ruled the world, it would be a better place than this, I can tell you!" God replies, "You do not have a clue about what you are saying. You have neither the power to manage the world nor the wisdom to comprehend what using that power is all about." God's point to Job is not simply that Job does not have God's omnipotence; it is that Job has no idea about what it means to be judge of all the earth. Job speaks of things he does not understand when he challenges God's administration and justice.

The description of Behemoth (40:15–24) leaves readers puzzled. What is this creature? Proposed interpretations include hippopotamus, elephant, crocodile, and whale. No single creature, however, fully fits the description. Behemoth eats grass like an ox, has strong muscles in its midsection, has a tail as stiff as a cedar, has strong thighs, has bones and limbs that are as strong as iron, eats in the mountains but also lies under the reeds in wetlands, takes shade under the lotus, and swims in the Jordan. A hippopotamus does not feed in the mountains or have a tail as strong as cedar. A crocodile has a strong tail but is not a herbivore and does not feed in the mountains. With some stretching of details, one might make this creature out to be an elephant (perhaps by taking "tail" to mean "trunk"), but it is hard to see how this creature could be a whale.

It is possible, in fact, that Behemoth is the human race. If Behemoth is not the "first" of the creatures of God chronologically, it must be first in rank. This place, of course, is held by humans. So understood, Behemoth is a composite for all the wildness and ferocity of the animal world and may specifically be the most beastly of all the animals, *Homo sapiens*.

Behemoth is thus natural but above any one natural animal, and it represents the fact that God alone manages nature and humanity in all their ferocity and beastliness. In this, Behemoth serves as a transition between the natural world

Clothe yourself in splendor

This demand (40:10) does not merely mean that Job should make himself look dazzling. To put on splendor and glory is to come in majesty to confront and overthrow all the powers of evil. It is similar to Psalm 145:5, where God's glorious splendor is linked to His mighty deeds to save His people.

Behemoth

It is hard to imagine that any single, specific animal is being described. *Behemoth,* in Hebrew, simply means "beasts" (that is, it is the plural form of the word for *beast*). Behemoth appears to be a kind of composite animal that represents the strength, domain, and independence of the animal world. It is wild, powerful, and free. Behemoth is not a supernatural creature, but it is more than one natural animal. It is a kind of conceptual being, a representative of animal wildness. The text tells us that it is the first of the great creatures of God (v. 19). In Genesis 1:20, the first living creatures are the fish and birds, but Behemoth is not some specific fish or fowl. Rather, Behemoth was "first" in that the animal world preceded the creation of humans. Similarly, when the text says that only Behemoth's "maker" can approach it, the meaning is that only God fully controls its wildness. This is the point that God repeatedly made to Job in all His descriptions of specific animals in the first speech.

of lions, goats, and horses and the description of the one beast that is truly supernatural: Leviathan.

The book devotes an enormous amount of space to Leviathan (41:1–34) without ever actually identifying it. Interpreters, of course, have sought to fill this gap, and the crocodile and the whale are the two candidates must commonly nominated for the title. But if it is difficult to imagine any animal that has all the characteristics ascribed to Behemoth, it is absolutely impossible to find any earthly creature like Leviathan.

The description of Leviathan in chapter 41 is staggering. No one can capture or tame him (vv. 1–6), but strangely enough, the text also asks, "Will he make many supplications to you?" Although this verse does not actually claim that Leviathan can speak, it is remarkable that even the possibility is mentioned. Leviathan is in a class by itself.

Leviathan is also invulnerable (vv. 7–8). He has "armor" (presumably scales) that is laid in a double coat (vv. 13, 15). His flesh is hard and tight (v. 23); even his belly is as hard and jagged as potsherds (v. 30). Neither sword, arrow, harpoon, club, slingstones, nor javelin has any affect on him, and the hardest metals do not bother him (vv. 26–29). His muscles are powerful (v. 12) and his neck mighty (v. 22). Leviathan dwells in the deep sea; and when he moves, he leaves a broad wake; and when he thrashes, the oceans seem to boil (vv. 31–32). Much of this could be taken as a hyperbolic description of the crocodile or whale, but further description makes even this interpretation unfeasible.

Leviathan breaths fire! Smoke comes out of his nostrils, and sparks fly when he sneezes. His breath can kindle coals (vv. 18–21). It is pointless to try to explain this as merely a metaphorical way of saying the Leviathan is ferocious; every other fierce creature is described in terms that although sometimes exaggerated are nevertheless recognizable and within the realm of nature. Leviathan is supernatural; Leviathan is a dragon.

Leviathan is the answer to one of the great mysteries of the book of Job: Whatever happened to Satan? After playing a prominent role in the first two chapters, Satan disappears entirely from the book, it would seem. No one mentions him in a speech although he is a critical part of the answer to the question of why so many troubles befell pious Job. One might wonder why God never told Job the real story behind his ordeal.

The answer is that God did tell Job; that is, at least He told Job what he needed to know. Leviathan is a depiction of Satan. The first speech described all the violent and powerful forces of nature that God alone can control, and it emphasized the dangerous creatures. Behemoth, as a composite beast and possibly also as a depiction of humanity, was a bridge between natural and supernatural ferocity. Leviathan completes the picture. He is the supernatural monster that is the image of chaotic and deadly forces. He is the representative of evil. The point God makes to Job is therefore clear: I alone can control Leviathan, the dragon of the Abyss.

The text does give us a hint that Leviathan is Satan. The translation of 41:10 is difficult, and versions differ regarding its interpretation, but it

Leviathan

The name *Leviathan* appears as *Lotan* in the myths of ancient Canaan, where he is a fierce dragon of the sea whom Baal must fight. Job 3:8 describes Leviathan as a demonic figure of the deep sea who is called up by sorcerers. Isaiah 27:1 says that one day the LORD will slay "Leviathan the gliding serpent" who is also "the monster of the sea." Psalm 74:13–14 similarly celebrates the power of God who crushes the head of Leviathan, the dragon of the waters. The term *Leviathan* in Psalm 104:26 seems to refer to ordinary whales, however. It appears that the same term was used both in reference to great (but ordinary) creatures of the sea and as a name for the great (supernatural or mythical) dragon. The sea of the dragon Leviathan is more of an abyss of death than the actual, physical ocean.

Job had challenged God's administration of the universe. He could not understand how God could be just and yet punish the innocent, as He had seemed to do in Job's case. God's answer is this: "I am the only one who can manage all the chaotic forces of life and who can bring about the ultimate triumph of righteousness, and I know what I am doing. If this has meant some suffering on your part, you must understand that this does not mean that I am unfair or that you have the right to challenge my justice. I will do what must be done to defeat Leviathan and all the powers of chaos and evil. This may sometimes require suffering on the part of the righteous, but I will bring all things to a just conclusion. Your role is simply to trust in my wisdom and goodness."

can be translated, "[Even] a fierce person should not try to arouse him. And who is he that presents himself before me?" This verse looks back to two verses in the book. The first part refers to Job 3:8, a verse that speaks of sorcerers who attempt to summon Leviathan (the same word for "arouse" is used in both texts). The second part, however, looks back to Job 1:6, when the "sons of God presented themselves" before God, using the same word for "present himself" in both texts. Thus, when God says, "And who is he that presents himself before me?" He is referring to the audacity of Satan/Leviathan who presents himself before God. The point is that sorcerers should not try to summon the demon Leviathan and that Leviathan/Satan has no real right to challenge God.

The book of Job has therefore reached an apocalyptic climax. The saintly Job has suffered almost unbearable pain and has had his faith stretched to the limit. But we have been given a look behind the curtain into heaven itself and have been allowed to see the real cause of Job's affliction. The suffering of the saints is comprehensible when one understands the true story. Meanwhile, the believer is expected to wait faithfully for God to execute His judgment and bring the terror of the great dragon to an end. For a while the dragon may seem to conquer, and the saints may have to flee into the wilderness (Rev. 12:13–17), but in the end the victory of God and of the right is certain. This is the message of Job. We may not understand all that God is doing, but He will slay the dragon. Only He is sufficient to manage human history and it does no good to second-guess Him.

One other aspect of God's answer bears noting. Throughout God's speeches, He did not say a word about the benefits Job had once enjoyed and now lost. He focused entirely on the power and person of God Himself as the only one who can control deadly forces. That is, the real benefit to serving God is in knowing God Himself. It is relationship with God and not a long life, great riches, or many children, that is the supreme benefit that comes from a life of faith.

- *God responded to Job by pointing out that Job*
- *was altogether incapable of managing the*
- *universe and bringing about the triumph of*
- *righteousness. In fact, Job did not even real-*
- *ize the magnitude of the situation. But God*
- *will bring about an end to the power of evil*
- *as embodied in the demonic figure of Levia-*
- *than.*

"And when the dragon saw that he was thrown down to the earth, he persecuted the woman who gave birth to the male child. . . . And the dragon was enraged with the woman, and went off to make war with the rest of her offspring, who keep the commandments of God and hold to the testimony of Jesus" (Rev. 12:13, 17, NASB).

JOB REPENTS (42:1–6)

In his response, Job paraphrases God's challenge to him (cp. 42:3 to 38:2, and 42:4 to 38:3 and 40:7). He is saying, "You are right. I had no idea what I was talking about." Job therefore repents. His repentance is not, however, what his friends imagined. He does not confess to having committed any sin that merited severe punishment, for he had committed none. Rather, he repents from his conclusion that God's severe treatment of him meant that God was not administering justice properly, and he humbles himself before a God who is truly great.

EPILOGUE (42:7–17)

God is angry. But to the discomfort and surprise of the three friends, His wrath is not directed at Job but at them. He is angry at the friends because they have not "spoken what is right." These champions of orthodoxy who upheld traditional theology in their passionate speeches confront an angry God who regards them as no better than liars! As a result they must make an enormous and expensive sacrifice (apparently each man had to bring seven bulls and seven rams) and suffer the humiliation of asking the man whom they had accused of being a reprobate to pray for them (vv. 7–9).

Job entered the story with substantially the same theology of retribution that his friends espoused. He, too, supposed that good and evil people got what they deserved. Job, however, correctly and courageously faced the fact that his theology had failed him; he had not deserved what had befallen him. The sin of the friends was not that their theology was altogether false but that they had refused to admit that Job had done nothing wrong. Supposing themselves to be defending God, they denied the truth. Job was angry but honest, and he quickly yielded when his broader vision of God enabled him to see that the triumph of God's justice over evil involved more than he had realized. There is truth in the theology of retribution, but it is not the whole truth. The greater truth is that God is bringing the chaotic story of the world to a just conclusion. This is the apocalyptic vision that allows Job to accept what has befallen him with renewed confidence in the goodness of God.

God then restores all of Job's fortunes to him and even gives him more children (vv. 10–17). We do not know why the three daughters are named but not the seven sons. It is doubtful that the names have profound significance; *Keren-happuch* simply means "bottle of eye-shadow"! It is certainly ironic that God repaid Job *double* for what he had lost (v. 10). This, according to Exodus 22:4, is the retribution that a thief is supposed to give to his victim!

Some may wonder if the restoration of Job's prosperity was necessary now that Job understood that knowing God is itself the great reward and that he need not fear that God's administration of justice has failed. God was not obligated to restore Job's wealth. Nevertheless, there is an important lesson here, too. God is involved in the large picture of administering the world and bringing evil to an end, but this does not mean that He is unconcerned about the needs and happiness of His people. Although He at times wounds, His delight is to give good things to those who fear Him. Furthermore, the prosperity of Job anticipates the final victory of God and the eternal joy of His people.

"If what he stole is actually found alive in his possession, whether an ox or a donkey or a sheep, he shall pay double" (Exod. 22:4, NASB).

Job's friends, who spoke falsely to maintain orthodox theology, found themselves facing an angry God. Job, who refused to lie for the sake of the theology of retribution but who quickly yielded when he saw that his vision of God was too small, was restored.

QUESTIONS TO GUIDE YOUR STUDY

1. What is the first question God asks of Job?

2. What is God's first command to Job?

3. What is God's point in His speech to Job?

4. Why was the Lord angry with Job's three friends?

The following is a collection of Broadman & Holman published reference sources used for this work. They are provided here to meet the reader's need for more specific information and/or an expanded treatment of the book of Job. All of these works will greatly aid in the reader's study, teaching, and presentation of Job. The accompanying annotations can be helpful in guiding the reader to the proper resources.

Alden, Robert L. Job (The New American Commentary), Vol. 11. . A theologically focused commentary on Job.

Cate, Robert L. *An Introduction to the Old Testament and Its Study.* An introductory work presenting background information, issues related to interpretation, and summaries of each book of the Old Testament.

Dockery, David S., Kenneth A. Mathews and Robert B. Sloan. *Foundations for Biblical Interpretation: A Complete Library of Tools and Resources.* A comprehensive introduction to matters relating to the composition and interpretation of the entire Bible. This work includes a discussion of the geographical, historical, cultural, religious, and political backgrounds of the Bible.

Farris, T. V. *Mighty to Save: A Study in Old Testament Soteriology.* A wonderful evaluation of many Old Testament passages that teach about salvation. This work makes a conscious attempt to apply Old Testament teachings to the Christian life.

Francisco, Clyde T. *Introducing the Old Testament.* Revised Edition. An introductory guide to each of the books of the Old Testament. This work includes a discussion on how to interpret the Old Testament.

Holman Bible Dictionary. An exhaustive, alphabetically arranged resource of Bible-related subjects. An excellent tool of definitions and other information on the people, places, things and events of the book of Job.

Holman Bible Handbook. A summary treatment of each book of the Bible that offers outlines, commentary on key themes and sections, illustrations, charts, maps, and full-color photos. This tool also provides an accent on broader theological teachings of the Bible.

Holman Book of Biblical Charts, Maps and Reconstructions. This easy-to-use work provides numerous color charts on various matters related to Bible content and background, maps of important events, and drawings of objects, buildings, and cities mentioned in the Bible.

Sandy, D. Brent and Ronald L. Giese Jr. *Cracking Old Testament Codes. A Guide to Interpreting the Literary Genres of the Old Testament.* This book is designed to make scholarly discussions available to preachers and teachers.

Smith, Ralph L. *Old Testament Theology: Its History, Method and Message.* A comprehensive treatment of various issues relating to Old Testament theology. Written for university and seminary students, ministers, and advanced lay teachers.

SHEPHERD'S NOTES

SHEPHERD'S NOTES